SIMPLY GOOD
GOOD
bread

Delicious home-baked recipes for everyone

Peter Sidwell

SIMPLY GOOD bread

Delicious home-baked recipes for everyone

Peter Sidwell

SIMON &
SCHUSTER
ILLUSTRATED

London · New York · Sydney · Toronto

A CBS COMPANY

First published in Great Britain by Peter Sidwell/RMC Brainwave, 2009

This revised edition published by Simon & Schuster UK Ltd, 2011
A CBS COMPANY

1 3 5 7 9 10 8 6 4 2

SIMON & SCHUSTER
ILLUSTRATED BOOKS
Simon & Schuster UK Ltd
222 Gray's Inn Road
London
WC1X 8HB

www.simonandschuster.co.uk

Editorial director: Francine Lawrence
Project editor: Abi Waters
Designer: Geoff Fennell
Photography: Richard Faulks
Cover photography: William Shaw
Production manager: Katherine Thornton
Commercial director: Ami Richards

A CIP catalogue record for this book is available from the British Library

ISBN 978-0-85720-313-7

Printed and bound in China
Colour reproduction by Dot Gradations Ltd, UK

RECIPE NOTES:

All teaspoons and tablespoons are level.

Both metric and imperial measurements have been given in all recipes.
Use one set of measurements only and not a mixture of both.

All cooking times are approximate and will vary in accordance with the
type of cooker hob, conventional or fan oven used.

Please be advised this book includes recipes where nuts have been used.

Eggs should be medium unless otherwise stated.

Fresh herbs should be used unless otherwise stated. If unavailable use
dried herbs as an alternative, but halve the quantities stated.

Contents

The joy of bread

The success of my first book, **Simply Good Taste**, encouraged me to write **Simply Good Bread**. It is packed with dozens of creative, yet easy-to-follow bread recipes to suit every mealtime and occasion – from a humble lunch or family picnic to a special dinner party.

I always cook with the best kitchen equipment and the best local ingredients that I can afford. As my grandmother used to say – buy cheap, buy twice…

I love nothing more than making bread by hand, it's very therapeutic and it gives me time to think about things. To be honest, making bread is one of those things where you get exactly what you put in – so, if you put lots of time and effort into it you will really taste the difference.

If you are anything like me though, life is hectic, busy and rushed, so a breadmaker can really help you out with putting fresh bread on the table. I use my breadmaker often when I don't have the time or the space in my kitchen for breadmaking by hand, so pull that breadmaker out of the cupboard and start using it even if it's just to make a dough.

I hope you feel inspired to have a go at making lots of my favourite loaves.

Happy breadmaking!

Don't be fooled by the millstones! I haven't got the time or the energy to grind my own flour, but it made a great shot for the book.

Chapter One
Basic bread

Ingredients

Using a breadmaker

Making dough in a breadmaker

Basic bread recipes

Making bread by hand

Homemade bread – the best!

One of my favourite memories from boyhood is tearing into the house from a game of football and cutting myself a thick slice of homemade bread. Still warm from the oven, it tasted like nothing else on earth.

Twenty years on, **Simply Good Bread** celebrates my continuing love affair with this most versatile of foods. Delicious, full of goodness and great fun to make, homemade bread should be at the heart of every family household.

Never made bread before? Let me show you how. This section is your own personal toolkit, helping you to make and bake basic loaves. From just three main ingredients – flour, yeast and water – you can make an array of amazing breads. Try a simple wholemeal loaf, a crusty baguette or a batch of white rolls. Always use a good-quality bread flour and let your breadmaker, or your hands, do the rest. When you are more confident and practised, try a challenging ciabatta or a flavoursome focaccia.

Ingredients

When you have mastered the art of making a good solid, plain bread dough, you can then begin your culinary adventure with baking bread. Different flours; yeast or no yeast; flavours and ingredients – the list of possibilities really goes on and on.

I love bread because it is so versatile and it will embrace and welcome so many different flavours – just open the cupboard doors and take your pick. Sometimes that will even dictate what kind of bread you are going to make – it's no good saying I want to make this bread or that bread if the ingredients aren't in the cupboard. Often the best breads are born out of what you have in the storecupboard needing to be used up and not what a recipe dictates you need!

So, start by keeping it simple and just experiment with different flours – take note of the way it will change the texture and density of the resulting bread. If you want to make a heavy bread, such as sourdough, you would use a high-gluten flour. If you want to make a soft bread like a family white or a soft brioche bun you would use a bread flour – it depends on the percentage of gluten in the flour.

Next, move on to the yeast – to use or not to use, dried or fresh, those are your options, all of which will give you very different breads. It all depends on personal taste, and the only way you'll get to understand it and form an opinion is by experimenting and trying out different combinations.

Liquid is the other key ingredient – usually it's water, but it can sometimes be joined by oil and/or milk or yogurt to get a completely different kind of loaf.

Lastly, there's the whole wealth of other flavours and ingredients you could add to mix it up a little. Really, the sky's the limit here.

Read on for more information on these different elements of breadmaking and how making a few changes here and there can hugely alter the bread you produce in the kitchen.

Flour

Flour is the backbone of good breadmaking. There is a vast array of different types of flour out there on the market to choose from. As with cooking, different flour suits different breads. Here's a quick rundown of the different types of flour and how they are best used.

Strong white bread flour – a flour with a high protein content that has had the bran and wheatgerm removed during milling. Ideal for bread made by hand or in a breadmaker and all types of yeast cookery, Yorkshire puddings, pizza bases and puff pastry.

Wholemeal – 100% extraction, made from the whole-wheat grain with nothing added or taken away. It gives a much coarser texture with a 'nutty' flavour.

Brown – contains about 85% of the original grain and is usually a mix of white and wholemeal flours. This produces a lighter bread than a wholemeal, but still retains the 'nutty' flavour.

Granary flour – brown or wholemeal flour with added malted grains for a distinctive nutty flavour and seedy texture.

Flour mixes/pre-packed mixes – ready-prepared mixes of flour with other ingredients which help you make bread more quickly. You can find these at all major supermarkets.

Rye – this flour has a very low gluten content, which gives rye bread its dense, chewy texture.

Gluten-free flour – this is a fairly new product on the market and is often made up of different flours like potato, chickpea and rice flour. These days you can buy many different gluten-free flours from delis, supermarkets and health-food shops.

The important thing is to make sure you read the label and ensure any flour that you use is suitable for breadmaking as this means it will have a high protein content. When water is added to flour during baking these proteins then go on to make gluten, which really becomes the building blocks of the structure of the bread.

Yeast

Yeast is the raising agent used in the process of breadmaking. I use both dried yeast and fresh yeast, it really depends on what you have available to you. It is very important to weigh yeast out accurately as it can very easily affect the end result of the bread if too much or too little is added.

Dried yeast – this needs to be soaked in liquid with some sugar added to it before it can be used. After 15–20 minutes left in a warm place, the yeasty liquid should be frothing and bubbling.

Fast-action/easy-blend yeast – can be added directly to the flour without being soaked first. It is very convenient to use as the dough will only need one rise during the proving time. It is important to remember that the granules are much smaller than dried yeast, so if you are swapping one for the other it is not possible to use the same amount like for like.

Fresh yeast – not so readily available any more, but if you can get hold of it, it should be wrapped in paper and kept in an air-tight container to prevent it going stale. When using fresh yeast always remember you need to use twice as much fresh to dried.

Starter dough

If you're going to make a starter, that means you've got the bug for making great artisan breads! Starter doughs are generally used as a way of giving the yeast a head start so that when the other bread ingredients have been added it has already begun to do its job.

There seems to be a lot of mystery surrounding starters for use in sourdoughs – a lot of bakers are very precious about how they do it, but not me, I want to keep it

simple and easy to do at home or at work. Simply mix the ingredients together and let the science bit take over. There are natural yeasts found in flour, so if you give it what it needs to thrive it should come to life and do the job of rising your bread. It will also help develop large air pockets in your bread as well as a fantastic crust.

Sourdough-based bread is great for making on the weekend ready to serve you for the coming week as it keeps quite well for at least a week and makes great toast or crostini.

Adding flavour

Bread is a great carrier of flavours and ingredients. Just have a look in your fridge and see if there is a pot of olives, pesto or cheese that needs using up and knead them into a basic bread dough – hey presto, you've got a great flavoured bread.

When adding nuts I always roast the nuts in the oven or on a low heat in a frying pan for a few minutes to bring out the nutty flavour. When they are ready I also season with a little sea salt and a tiny bit of runny honey before adding them to the dough.

So, make a start by adding one or two flavours to your basic dough, such as garlic and herbs, and then away you go – experiment with different flavour combinations and be led by your palate. Don't forget, the flavour combination might not always work, but you've had fun along the way and a failed bread attempt is never wasted when there are ducks at the pond to feed!

Some great flavour combos:
- red onion and Cheddar cheese
- pesto and Parmesan
- olive, feta and rosemary
- cumin and coriander seeds
- thyme and courgette
- pancetta and mozzarella
- smoked cheese and chive
- sun-dried tomatoes and mozzarella
- anchovy and roasted onion

Using a breadmaker

Of all the many modern kitchen appliances, the breadmaker is my personal favourite. Lightweight, compact and time-saving, it makes delicious fresh bread whenever you need it. Whether you are an experienced baker looking for new recipe challenges or a novice excited by the thought of making a loaf for the first time, your breadmaker is more than just a labour-saving device – it is a friend in the kitchen.

People are sometimes surprised by just how easy it is to use a breadmaker – perhaps remembering school cookery classes and all the effort and time needed to make a loaf by hand! But once you've decided on a recipe, simply put all your ingredients into the breadmaker, close the lid, press a couple of buttons and stand back and let it do all the work. Yes, it really is that straightforward.

I may be used to making 20kg (44lb) of bread dough at a time, but I still use my breadmaker at home, usually once or twice a week, for all sorts of things.

If your breadmaker has a timer you can set it to bake a loaf overnight, just in time for breakfast. Most breadmakers even have a dispenser for adding nuts, raisins or chocolate chips etc. during cooking and they also allow you to select the size of loaf and type of crust.

After use, simply wipe down with a soft damp cloth, ready for the next loaf. Look after your breadmaker and it will keep you and your family in fresh bread for many years to come.

To make a loaf in a breadmaker

It couldn't be simpler. Familiarise yourself with the manufacturers' instructions for your make of breadmaker. Follow their guidelines as to the order in which you put the ingredients into the bread pan – liquid or dry ingredients first, for example. Then set your machine to the setting required – use the suggestions and recipes in this book, or the manufacturers' instructions will no doubt have a couple of basic recipes, to get yourself used to breadmaking by machine. When the bread is ready, remove immediately from the pan and leave to cool. It couldn't be simpler.

Making dough in a breadmaker

All recipes can be made either in a breadmaker or by hand, but some recipes will need to be finished off by hand and baked in the oven. In these cases you will just need to make the dough in your breadmaker. Don't panic! After putting your ingredients into the bread pan, simply press the 'dough' button and remove when ready. Then, follow the recipe instructions for using the dough to create different types of loaves, before baking in a conventional oven or even on a barbecue.

If you are like me and love rolling your sleeves up and kneading dough, a breadmaker can really come into its own here. Set it to make the dough only and then you can scoop it out onto your work surface and make it into all kinds of things – you don't want the machine to have all the fun, do you?

Handling dough

Don't be afraid to handle dough – it's tactile, fun, versatile and therapeutic. If your dough is too sticky simply dust your hands with a little flour. Relish the experience. Human beings have been handling dough for thousands of years. It's the backbone of civilisation; from the Greeks and Romans to the present day.

Basic bread recipes

Here is a selection of basic recipes; these will make up the foundation of your breadmaking adventure. For me, the key to great cooking is to have a little confidence and faith in what you are doing. Try to master these recipes and get used to touching and feeling the dough, so you know by feel and sight that the dough is ready for you to step in and start creating mouth-watering loaves of bread. If you are using a breadmaker, then use the settings suggested below for each recipe. If you are baking by hand, then ignore the breadmaker setting instructions below, use the oven temperature suggested instead and follow the basic instructions for baking by hand on page 27.

Basic white dough

Once you've got a basic dough mastered you can start to make all kinds of treats.

INGREDIENTS

500g (1lb) strong white bread flour

1¼ tsp salt

1 tsp fast-action/easy-blend yeast

1½ tsp granulated sugar

300ml (½ pint) water

BREADMAKER SETTING

Basic/Normal

OR BY HAND

200°C (400°F), gas mark 6 for 30–40 minutes

Enriched loaf

This loaf is great as a brioche or even add in chocolate, dried fruit and nuts to make a panettone loaf.

INGREDIENTS

500g (1lb) strong white bread flour

1 tsp salt

1 tsp fast-action/easy-blend yeast

25g (1oz) granulated sugar

300ml (½ pint) water

25g (1oz) butter

1 egg

BREADMAKER SETTING

Basic/Normal

OR BY HAND

200°C (400°F), gas mark 6 for 30–40 minutes

Wholemeal loaf

Wholemeal flour has a wonderful dense, nutty kind of flavour and is a great source of fibre.

INGREDIENTS

500g (1lb) plain wholemeal flour

1¼ tsp salt

1 tsp fast-action/easy-blend yeast

1½ tsp granulated sugar

380ml (13fl oz) water

25g (1oz) butter/25ml (1fl oz) oil

BREADMAKER SETTING

Wholewheat

OR BY HAND

200°C (400°F), gas mark 6 for 30–40 minutes

Brown loaf

A good brown loaf is always needed – it seems to keep a bit longer, too.

INGREDIENTS

500g (1lb) brown flour

1¼ tsp salt

1 tsp fast-action/easy-blend yeast

1½ tsp granulated sugar

350ml (12 fl oz) water

25g (1oz) butter/25ml (1fl oz) oil

BREADMAKER SETTING

Basic/Normal

OR BY HAND

200°C (400°F), gas mark 6 for 30–40 minutes

Baguette

Create steam to make a nice crusty baguette by putting ice cubes in a tin at the bottom of the oven as you bake.

INGREDIENTS

125g (4oz) strong white bread flour

490g (15½ oz) overnight sponge*

1 tsp salt

BREADMAKER SETTING

Pizza/Dough

OR BY HAND

200°C (400°F), gas mark 6 for 30–40 minutes

50/50

Fool the kids into thinking they are having white bread!

INGREDIENTS

250g (8oz) plain wholemeal flour

250g (8oz) strong white bread flour

1¼ tsp salt

1 tsp fast-action/easy-blend yeast

1½ tsp granulated sugar

350ml (12fl oz) water

25g (1oz) butter/25ml (1fl oz) oil

BREADMAKER SETTING

Wholewheat

OR BY HAND

200°C (400°F), gas mark 6 for 30–40 minutes

Ciabatta/Focaccia

Italian breads are great for mopping up good olive oil.

INGREDIENTS

125g (4oz) strong white bread flour

490g (15½ oz) overnight sponge*

1 tsp salt

25g (1oz) butter/25ml (1fl oz) oil

BREADMAKER SETTING

Pizza/Dough

OR BY HAND

200°C (400°F), gas mark 6 for 30–40 minutes

Naan

Naan breads are my favourite part of an Indian meal.

INGREDIENTS

225g (7½oz) strong white bread flour

490g (15½ oz) overnight sponge*

1 tsp salt

25g (1oz) granulated sugar

25g (1oz) butter/25ml (1fl oz) oil

BREADMAKER SETTING

Pizza/Dough

OR BY HAND

200°C (400°F), gas mark 6 for 30–40 minutes

*To make an overnight sponge

Simply mix 250g (8oz) strong white bread flour, 225ml (7½ fl oz) water and 1 tsp fast-action/easy-blend yeast in a bowl. Cover with a tea towel secured with an elastic band and leave for 12 hours.

Basic bread

Making bread by hand

Making bread by hand is really simple – it's a very tactile process and I find it really therapeutic. It has to be one of the most rewarding jobs in the kitchen. I always feel a real sense of achievement when I look at what I've made and I am sure you will feel the same too. It's a great way of enjoying spending time in your kitchen. Your hands play a big part in the kneading process and making the dough so you can't be afraid of rolling your sleeves up and getting stuck in.

To bake bread by hand

The first thing to do is to weigh out your flour in a large bowl, add in your salt then the yeast and sugar, followed by your water and any other flavouring ingredients that have taken your fancy. Get your hands in the bowl and mix together until it forms a smooth dough. When it comes away from the bowl and onto your hand easily, transfer it to a lightly floured work surface. Continue to knead (see below) until smooth.

Return the dough to the bowl, cover and leave to prove in a warm place for 30–40 minutes or until it has doubled in size. Return the dough back to a floured work surface and knead and shape your desired loaf.

Place the bread on a baking tray or into a non-stick loaf tin and leave it somewhere warm to prove and double in size again before placing it into an oven preheated to 200°C (400°F), gas mark 6 for about 30 minutes, depending on the actual recipe you are following.

Kneading basics

Getting kneading right takes time and patience, and there's no other way than to just get stuck in with your hands and work some of your frustration of day-to-day life out on that dough!

Put the dough onto a lightly floured surface and begin by stretching the bread away from you with one hand whilst holding it with the other. Bring it back towards you, then continue to stretch it away and back until it becomes very smooth and pliable without adding any extra flour. It should take about 5–10 minutes.

To check if your loaf is cooked

If your loaf is cooking on a baking tray or bread stone then it should be cooked when it has turned golden on top and sounds hollow when tapped underneath. If your loaf is cooking in a loaf tin, you will need to carefully slide it out of the tin to tap it underneath and check if it sounds hollow or not. If it is not quite cooked, then return it to the oven for a further 10 minutes and check again.

Chapter Two
Everyday bread

Soda bread with spring onion

French onion bread

Super seed bread

Roasted garlic & rosemary bread

Gluten-free bread with nuts & seeds

Bagels with sun-blushed tomato

Pitta with poppy seeds, carrots & raisins

Coffee, chocolate & roasted pine nut sweet bread

Cheese & Marmite bread

Pesto rolls

Dark German-style rye bread

Folded flatbread

Cumbrian whigg bread

Cider apple bread

Chestnut flour bread

Coriander & cumin bread

Easy living

Over the last couple of years or so I've noticed that people are re-examining what is really important to them. The mad scramble to work harder and longer just to buy bigger, better houses and cars seems to be on the way out. Like fashion, lifestyles and attitudes often come full circle.

Whether you live in the countryside or in the middle of a large city, it is easy to lose sight of the things that matter. Modern life is so demanding that it is all too easy to rush to the shop to grab a white sliced loaf without thinking.

Like intensively farmed chicken, mass-produced bread can't hold a candle to a homemade loaf in terms of taste and nutrition. With any kind of flour and an automatic breadmaker you can make a scrumptious loaf – like bread used to taste – in the time it takes you to drive to the shop.

Baking your own bread – part of a gradual return to the essentials of life – breathes life into every nook and cranny of your home. Set the timer on your breadmaker so the aroma of freshly baked bread wakes you up in the morning. Hmm... warm bread, creamy butter and fresh coffee! What better way to start your day?

Make everyday breads the backbone of your pantry – they're great for sandwiches, quick snacks and lighter meals.

Soda bread with spring onion

My nana was Irish and I have very fond memories of holidays in Ballymoney where some of my relatives still live and where I was introduced to soda bread. It's so easy to make – no proving, just mix and bake. It's the perfect partner to Irish stew and even better toasted the next day.

INGREDIENTS

450g (14oz) self-raising flour

1 tsp bicarbonate of soda

1 tsp salt

¼ tsp ground white pepper

1 bunch of spring onions

2 tbsp plain yogurt

50ml (2fl oz) oil or 50g (2oz) butter, melted

225ml (7½fl oz) milk

Here's how...

Sieve the flour, bicarbonate of soda, salt and white pepper into a bowl. Using a pair of kitchen scissors, cut the spring onions into the same bowl – use all parts of the onion, white and green.

Make a well in the middle of the flour and pour in the yogurt, oil or melted butter and the milk. Stir the mixture together and add more milk as required to form a soft dough.

To bake in a breadmaker

Line the bread pan with baking parchment to ensure the bread does not stick while baking. Place the dough into your parchment-lined pan and place on the bake only setting for 45 minutes.

To bake by hand

Preheat the oven to 180°C (350°F), gas mark 4.

Shape the dough into a smooth round loaf and place on a non-stick baking tray. Using a pair of kitchen scissors, cut a criss-cross into the middle of the bread about halfway into the loaf – this will open the bread out and allow it to cook evenly. Alternatively, bake in a 1kg (2lb) non-stick loaf tin for a more traditional loaf shape.

Bake in the preheated oven for 30 minutes until the loaf is golden on top and sounds hollow when tapped underneath.

French onion bread

I love French food, so if you are making the 'king of soups' just double up on the onions, garlic and vegetable stock for this hearty bread accompaniment.

INGREDIENTS

1 large white onion, thinly sliced

1 tbsp vegetable oil

1 garlic clove, crushed

1 tsp fresh thyme, chopped, plus some extra sprigs to garnish

600ml (1 pint) vegetable stock

2 tbsp French mustard

100g (3½oz) Swiss Gruyère cheese

Salt and freshly ground black pepper

For the dough

500g (1lb) strong white bread flour

1¼ tsp salt

1 tsp fast-action/easy-blend yeast

1½ tsp granulated sugar

300ml (½ pint) water

Here's how... To make the dough in a breadmaker

Place all of the dough ingredients into the bread pan following your manufacturers' instructions regarding the order of liquid/dry ingredients and set your machine to the dough/pizza setting.

To make the dough by hand

Place the flour and salt into a mixing bowl and mix together the yeast, sugar and water in a measuring jug. Pour the liquid into the dry ingredients and using your hands, mix together until it forms a dough and comes away from the bowl – it should take about 3–4 minutes. Transfer the dough onto a lightly floured work surface and knead (see basic instructions on page 27) for about 5–10 minutes. Transfer the dough back into the bowl, cover with cling film and leave in a warm place for 30–40 minutes to double in size. Scoop the bread back out and give it a simple knead for 1 minute.

To finish

Place the sliced onion into a medium-sized saucepan with the oil. Season the onion with salt and pepper to draw the water out of the onions and help them caramelise. Add the garlic to the onions along with the chopped thyme and cook gently until the onions turn golden (the more you cook them without burning the sweeter the onion flavour). Add the vegetable stock, boil to reduce the volume by half, then leave the onions to cool.

Turn the prepared dough out onto a lightly floured surface, roll it into a rectangle about 40 x 20cm (16 x 8in). Spread with the mustard and the onions. Roll the bread up from the short end and stand it on its end. Cover and leave the bread in a warm place to prove for about 30 minutes.

Preheat the oven to 200°C (400°F), gas mark 6 and line a baking tray with greaseproof paper.

Transfer the bread dough to the lined baking tray, rolled side up, and grate plenty of cheese on top. Add a few sprigs of fresh thyme to the top and leave to prove in a warm place for 20–30 minutes.

Bake the bread in the preheated oven for 30–40 minutes or until it is golden on top and sounds hollow when tapped underneath.

Super seed bread

I came up with this recipe so that I could have a couple of slices of toast that would last me well past lunchtime as I had a really busy day. The nuts and seeds release energy slowly all day long so you don't feel hungry.

INGREDIENTS

250g (8oz) strong white bread flour

100g (3½oz) plain wholemeal bread flour

75g (3oz) muesli

1 tbsp millet seeds

1 tbsp poppy seeds

1 tbsp pumpkin seeds

1 tbsp sunflower seeds

1 tsp of salt

1½ tsp fast-action/easy-blend yeast

1 tbsp runny honey

350ml (12fl oz) warm water

Here's how... To make the dough in a breadmaker

Place all of the ingredients, except the seeds, into the bread pan following your manufacturers' instructions regarding the order of liquid/dry ingredients. Place the seeds in the raisin/nut dispenser (if available) and set your machine to the light wholemeal setting. If you do not have a dispenser, when the machine indicates (with a beeping sound), add the seeds. When the cycle is complete, remove the dough. Knead for 1 minute to remove the air, cover and leave to rest for 10 minutes.

To make the dough by hand

Place both the flours, muesli, seeds and salt into a mixing bowl. Mix together the yeast, honey and water in a measuring jug. Pour the liquid into the dry ingredients and using your hands, mix together until it forms a dough and comes away from the bowl – it should take about 3–4 minutes. Transfer the dough onto a lightly floured work surface and knead (see basic instructions on page 27) for about 5–10 minutes. Return the dough back to the bowl, cover with cling film and leave in a warm place for 30–40 minutes to double in size. Scoop the bread back out and give it a simple knead for 1 minute.

To finish

Mould the dough into your desired loaf shape and place it onto a non-stick baking tray or place in a 1kg (2lb) non-stick loaf tin for a more traditional loaf shape. Leave the bread somewhere warm to prove for 20–30 minutes or until it has almost doubled in size. Preheat the oven to 200°C (400°F), gas mark 6.

Bake the bread in the preheated oven for about 30 minutes until it is golden on top and sounds hollow when tapped underneath.

Roasted garlic & rosemary bread

Everyone should have room for a rosemary plant in their garden. It's a hearty, robust herb that can bear tough British winters and suits all Mediterranean-style food. The flavours are perfect with roasted garlic.

INGREDIENTS

1 whole bulb of garlic

50ml (2fl oz) olive oil

2 sprigs of fresh rosemary

For the dough

500g (1lb) strong white bread flour

1¼ tsp salt

1 tsp fast-action/easy-blend yeast

1½ tsp granulated sugar

300ml (½ pint) water

Here's how...

Preheat the oven to 150°C (300°F), gas mark 2.

Place the bulb of garlic into an ovenproof dish and drizzle with the olive oil. Roast in the preheated oven for 1 hour until the garlic goes really soft and sweet. Remove the garlic from the oven and leave it to cool.

To make the dough in a breadmaker

Place all of the dough ingredients into the bread pan following your manufacturers' instructions regarding the order of liquid/dry ingredients and set your machine to the dough/pizza setting.

To make the dough by hand

Place the flour and salt into a mixing bowl and mix together the yeast, sugar and water in a measuring jug. Pour the liquid into the dry ingredients and using your hands, mix together until it forms a dough and comes away from the bowl – it should take about 3–4 minutes. Transfer the dough onto a lightly floured work surface and knead (see basic instructions on page 27) for about 5–10 minutes. Return the dough back to the bowl, cover with cling film and place in a warm place for 30–40 minutes to double in size. Scoop the bread back out and give it a simple knead for 1 minute.

To finish

Turn out the dough and press it into a flat circle. Pull the cooled garlic bulb apart and squeeze each clove out of its skin onto the dough. Strip the rosemary leaves from their stalks and sprinkle them on top. Gently knead the dough – enough to incorporate the garlic and rosemary into the bread but taking care not to break up all the garlic as you want the cloves to stay as whole as possible.

Preheat the oven to 200°C (400°F), gas mark 6.

Mould the bread into a bloomer shape (a long oval), transfer it to a non-stick baking tray, cover and leave it to prove for about 30 minutes. Cook in the preheated oven for 20–25 minutes until it is golden on top and sounds hollow when tapped underneath.

Gluten-free bread with nuts & seeds

Gluten-free bread is a tough culinary nut to crack as without gluten it is difficult to hold the air in the loaf. This loaf is beautiful eaten fresh but quickly goes rock hard. My advice is to bake it, let it cool, cut into slices, freeze and toast from frozen when needed.

INGREDIENTS

1 tbsp linseeds

1 tbsp pumpkin seeds

1 tbsp sesame seeds

1 tbsp millet seeds

1 tbsp walnuts, chopped

450g (14oz) gluten-free flour

1 tsp salt, plus a little extra for the nuts and seeds

1½ tsp fast-action/easy-blend yeast

1 tsp granulated sugar or runny honey

350ml (12fl oz) water

1 tsp cider vinegar

4 tsp vegetable oil

2 eggs

Here's how...

Before making the bread, roast the seeds and nuts to enhance their nutty flavour. Sprinkle with a little salt and leave to cool. I suggest you buy a packet of each of the seeds and nuts and cook them all together. When cooled, store them in an airtight container and use them as needed as they are great for baking or stirring through salads to give texture and flavour.

To bake in a breadmaker

Place all the ingredients into the bread pan following the manufacturers' instructions regarding the order of liquid/dry ingredients and set your machine to the gluten-free setting with dark crust.

To bake by hand

Place the gluten-free flour and salt into a mixing bowl and mix together the yeast, sugar, water, vinegar, oil and eggs in a measuring jug. Pour the liquid into the dry ingredients and also add the seeds and nuts. Using your hands, mix together until it forms a dough and comes away from the bowl – it should take about 3–4 minutes. Transfer the dough onto a lightly floured work surface and knead (see basic instructions on page 27) for about 5–10 minutes. Return the dough back to the bowl, cover with cling film and leave in a warm place for 30–40 minutes to double in size.

Preheat the oven to 180°C (350°F), gas mark 4 and line a 1kg (2lb) loaf tin with baking parchment.

Pour the mixture into the prepared tin and bake it in the preheated oven for 30 minutes until it is golden on top. To check if it is cooked, carefully slide the loaf out of the tin and tap the underneath. If it sounds hollow it is cooked, if not, return it to the oven for another 10 minutes.

Bagels with sun-blushed tomato

I love the texture of bagels. Nowadays, they are a mobile food being both convenient and versatile and also perfect for all sorts of fillings, or being toasted like mini pizzas. These sun-blushed tomato bagels are perfect served with lashings of cream cheese, black pepper and fresh basil leaves.

INGREDIENTS

400g (13oz) strong white bread flour

1 tsp fast-action/easy-blend yeast

1 tsp dried oregano

1 tsp salt

1 tbsp granulated sugar

1 tbsp olive oil

225ml (7½fl oz) water

10 sun-blushed tomatoes

1 egg yolk (optional)

Here's how... To make the dough in a breadmaker

Place all of the ingredients, except the tomatoes and the egg yolk, into the bread pan following your manufacturers' instructions regarding the order of liquid/dry ingredients. Place the tomatoes in the raisin/nut dispenser (if available) and set your machine to the basic raisin dough setting. If you do not have a nut/raisin dispenser, when the machine indicates (with a beeping sound), add the tomatoes. When the cycle is complete, remove the dough. Give it a simple knead for 1 minute, cover and leave to rest for 10 minutes.

To make the dough by hand

Place all of the ingredients except the egg yolk in a mixing bowl and using one hand, mix the ingredients together to form a dough. Transfer the dough onto a lightly floured work surface and knead (see basic instructions on page 27) for about 5–10 minutes. Return the dough back to the bowl, cover with cling film and leave to prove for 30–40 minutes in a warm place.

To finish

Divide the dough into nine equal portions. Working quickly, shape each into a smooth ball. Punch a hole in the centre and pull gently to produce a 5cm (2in) hole. Place the bagels on a large greased baking sheet. Cover and leave to prove for 20 minutes (start timing after the first bagel is shaped).

Preheat the oven to 180°C (350°F), gas mark 4 and line a baking tray with non-stick baking parchment.

Bring a large shallow pan of water to the boil and place 3–4 bagels in at a time. Cook for 1–2 minutes on each side then transfer them to the lined baking tray. Brush with an egg yolk wash, if desired, and bake in the preheated oven for 20 minutes until they are golden on top and sound hollow when tapped underneath.

Pitta with poppy seeds, carrots & raisins

Pitta breads are universally popular. Use them with dips to start any party or meal – let everyone just tuck in. My one-year-old daughter likes to dip everyone's bread for them, only then can they eat! This recipe is for a basic pitta but I wanted to show you another use as a healthy sandwich.

INGREDIENTS

2 tbsp olive oil

2 tbsp honey

2 tbsp orange juice

4 washed and peeled carrots

50g (2oz) raisins

2 tbsp poppy seeds

A few sprigs of fresh coriander

Houmous, to serve

For the dough

500g (1lb) strong white
bread flour

1¼ tsp salt

1 tsp fast-action/easy-blend
yeast

1½ tsp granulated sugar

300ml (½ pint) water

2 tbsp olive oil

Here's how... To make the dough in a breadmaker

Place all of the dough ingredients into the bread pan following the manufacturers' instructions regarding the order of liquid/dry ingredients and set your machine to the dough/pizza setting.

To make the dough by hand

Place the flour and salt into a mixing bowl and mix together the yeast, sugar, water and oil in a measuring jug. Pour the liquid into the dry ingredients and using your hands, mix together until it forms a dough and comes away from the bowl – it should take about 3–4 minutes. Transfer the dough onto a lightly floured work surface and knead (see basic instructions on page 27) for about 5–10 minutes. Return the dough back to the bowl, cover with cling film and leave in a warm place for 30–40 minutes to double in size. Scoop the bread back out and give it a simple knead for 1 minute.

To finish

Preheat the oven to 200°C (400°F), gas mark 6 and line a baking tray with non-stick baking parchment.

Turn the dough onto a lightly floured surface and divide into 12 pieces. Roll out the portions into oval pitta shapes, around ½cm (¼in) thick. Transfer the shaped pittas to the prepared baking tray. Bake in the preheated oven for about 5–10 minutes. (If the weather permits cook them on the barbecue grill – you'll get a fantastic colour and flavour.)

To make the salad: place the oil, honey and orange juice in a mixing bowl and whisk together lightly. Grate the carrots into the bowl over the dressing. Add the raisins, poppy seeds and coriander and mix well to ensure the salad is dressed.

Cut each pitta bread in half, open it up slightly to create a pocket, spread with a little houmous and fill with as much of the salad as you can.

Coffee, chocolate & roasted pine nut sweet bread

I love café culture and built my business, Good Taste, around great-tasting coffee. I am always looking out for the ultimate companion for my espresso, latte or cappuccino. This bread comes pretty close to perfection.

INGREDIENTS

1 tsp fast-action/easy-blend yeast

200g (7oz) strong white bread flour

200g (7oz) pasta flour

1 tsp cocoa powder

½ tsp salt

⅔ tbsp granulated sugar

1 shot of good strong coffee (1 espresso or 2 tsp instant coffee dissolved in a splash of hot water)

140ml (4½fl oz) milk

1 egg

2 egg yolks

Zest of half an orange

75g (3oz) butter, at room temperature

50g (2oz) roasted pine nuts (baked in an oven for 10 minutes at 150°C (300°F), gas mark 2 until golden)

125g (4oz) dark chocolate chunks

Here's how... To make the dough in a breadmaker

Place the yeast in the bread pan first and then all the remaining ingredients, except the roasted pine nuts and dark chocolate chunks, following the manufacturers' instructions regarding the order of liquid/dry ingredients. Set your machine to the dough/pizza setting.

To make the dough by hand

Place the yeast in a large mixing bowl followed by the flours, cocoa powder, salt, sugar, coffee, milk, egg and yolks, orange zest and butter. Using one hand, mix the ingredients together until it forms a dough. Transfer the dough onto a lightly floured work surface and knead (see basic instructions on page 27) for about 5–10 minutes. Return the dough back to the bowl, cover with cling film and leave it in a warm place for 30–40 minutes to double in size.

To finish

Turn the dough out onto a lightly floured surface. Knock the dough back gently, press it flat and sprinkle over the roasted pine nuts and the chocolate chunks. Fold the dough back onto itself a few times so the nuts and chocolate run through the dough evenly.

Shape and place the dough in a round baking tin lined with parchment and leave to prove for at least 30 minutes or until it doubles in size. Preheat the oven to 180°C (350°F), gas mark 4.

Bake the loaf in the preheated oven for 30 minutes until it is golden on top. To check if it is cooked, carefully slide the loaf out of the tin and tap the underneath. If it sounds hollow it is cooked, if not, return it to the oven for another 10 minutes.

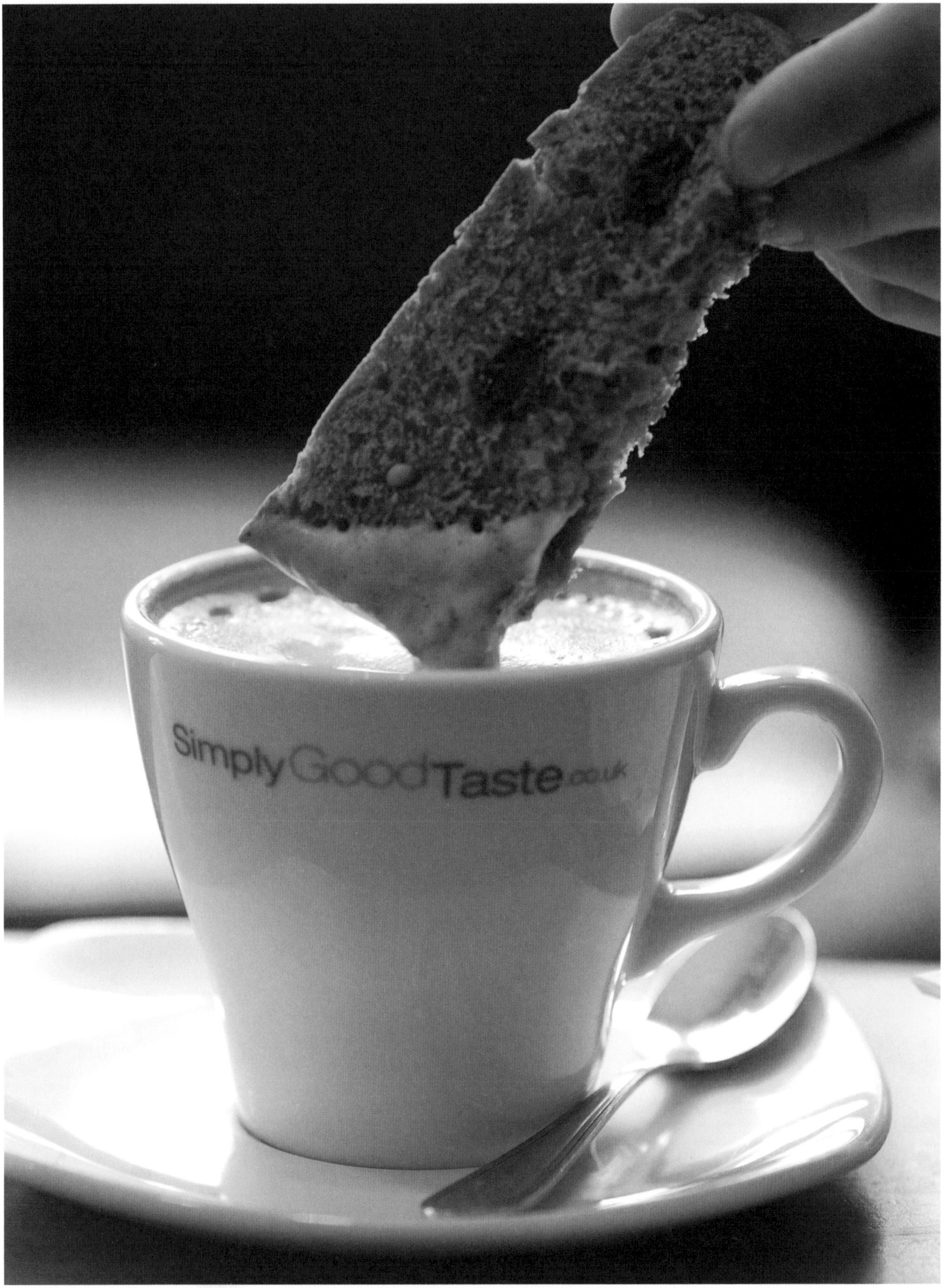
SimplyGoodTaste.co.uk

Cheese & Marmite bread

Marmite is my desert island food. I was fed it as a kid and I take a jar with me everywhere I go – I pack it along with my passport. On my first date with my future wife I asked if she liked Marmite. She said yes so I knew we would make it.

INGREDIENTS
2 tbsp Marmite

100g (3½oz) good-quality English mature Cheddar, grated

For the dough
500g (1lb) strong white bread flour

1¼ tsp salt

1 tsp fast-action/easy-blend yeast

1½ tsp granulated sugar

300ml (½ pint) water

Here's how... To make the dough in a breadmaker
Place all of the dough ingredients into the bread pan following the manufacturers' instructions regarding the order of liquid/dry ingredients and set your machine to the dough/pizza setting.

To make the dough by hand
Place the flour and salt into a mixing bowl and mix together the yeast, sugar and water in a measuring jug. Pour the liquid into the dry ingredients and using your hands, mix together until it forms a dough and comes away from the bowl – it should take about 3–4 minutes. Transfer the dough onto a lightly floured work surface and knead (see basic instructions on page 27) for about 5–10 minutes. Return the dough back to the bowl, cover with cling film and leave in a warm place to double in size. Scoop the bread back out and give it a simple knead for 1 minute.

To finish
Turn the dough onto a lightly floured surface and roll into a rectangle about 40 x 20cm (16 x 8in). Spread the Marmite on top and sprinkle with the cheese. Roll the far side of the dough towards you to make a Swiss roll and place, with the folded edge underneath, on a baking tray lined with parchment paper. Cover and leave the dough to prove for about 30 minutes or until it doubles in size. Meanwhile, preheat the oven to 200°C (400°F), gas mark 6.

Bake the bread in the preheated oven for about 25–30 minutes until it is golden on top and sounds hollow when tapped underneath.

Pesto rolls

I sent Dan, one of my chefs, travelling around Italy so he would get my passion for Italian food. He got it! He and I developed this recipe together after seeing something similar in Venice. Serve as an alternative to garlic bread when eating pasta or swap for a sandwich.

INGREDIENTS

500g (1lb) strong white
　bread flour

1¼ tsp salt

1 tsp fast-action/easy-blend
　yeast

1½ tsp granulated sugar

300ml (½ pint) water

25ml (1fl oz) oil

4 tbsp pesto

Sea salt

Here's how... To make the dough in a breadmaker

Place all of the ingredients, except the pesto and salt, into the bread pan following the manufacturers' instructions regarding the order of liquid/dry ingredients and set your machine to the dough/pizza setting.

To make the dough by hand

Place the flour and salt into a mixing bowl and mix together the yeast, sugar, water and oil in a measuring jug. Pour the liquid into the dry ingredients and using your hands, mix together until it forms a dough and comes away from the bowl – it should take about 3–4 minutes. Transfer the dough onto a lightly floured work surface and knead (see basic instructions on page 27) for about 5–10 minutes. Return the dough back to the bowl, cover with cling film and leave in a warm place for 30–40 minutes to double in size. Scoop the bread back out and give it a simple knead for 1 minute.

To finish

Turn the dough onto a lightly floured surface and roll into a 40 x 30cm (16 x 12in) rectangle. Spread the pesto on top and roll the far side of the dough towards you to make a Swiss roll. Cut the dough into 4cm (1½in) slices and transfer to a parchment-lined baking tray. Sprinkle with a little sea salt, cover and leave to prove for 20 minutes. Meanwhile, preheat the oven to 200°C (400°F), gas mark 6.

Bake the rolls in the preheated oven for 20 minutes until they are golden on top and sound hollow when tapped underneath.

Dark German-style rye bread

A savoury bread with a distinctive flavour. A great starter when toasted and served with smoked salmon, cream cheese, capers and parsley. This recipe is an ongoing development between myself and Dan, one of my chefs who shares my passion for baking bread.

INGREDIENTS

300g (10oz) rye flour

200g (7oz) strong wholemeal bread flour

1 tsp of salt

400ml (14fl oz) water

1 tsp fast-action/easy-blend yeast

2 tsp black treacle

Here's how... To bake in a breadmaker

Use the rye blade. Place all of the ingredients into the bread pan following the manufacturers' instructions regarding the order of liquid/dry ingredients and set your machine to the rye setting.

To bake by hand

Firstly, boil the kettle and whisk together a cup of the dark rye flour and a cup of boiling water and leave it to one side to cool.

Place the wholemeal flour, the remaining rye flour and the salt in a mixing bowl. Add the wet rye mixture to the flour along with the water, yeast and treacle. Using your hands, mix together until it forms a dough and comes away from the bowl – it should take about 3–4 minutes. Transfer the dough to a lightly floured work surface and knead (see basic instructions on page 27) for about 5–10 minutes. Return the dough back to the bowl, cover with cling film and leave in a warm place for 30–40 minutes to double in size. Scoop the bread back out and give it a simple knead for 1 minute.

Place the bread dough in a 1kg (2lb) non-stick loaf tin and leave to prove for 30 minutes or until it has almost doubled in size. Meanwhile, preheat the oven to 180°C (350°F), gas mark 4.

Bake the bread in the preheated oven for 30–40 minutes until it is golden on top. To check if it is cooked, carefully slide the loaf out of the tin and tap the underneath. If it sounds hollow it is cooked, if not, return it to the oven for another 10 minutes.

Folded flatbread

I came across this style of flatbread in the back streets of Florence where there was an endless selection of fillings all loosely based around the great Italian antipasti – my favourite kind of sandwich. Here is my version.

INGREDIENTS

500g (1lb) strong white bread flour

1¼ tsp salt

1 tsp fast-action/easy-blend yeast

1½ tsp granulated sugar

300ml (½ pint) water

To serve

Roasted pumpkin slices, mozzarella cheese and salad leaves

Air-dried ham, capers and rocket leaves dressed with olive oil and a little lemon juice

Here's how... To make the dough in a breadmaker

Place all of the dough ingredients into the bread pan following the manufacturers' instructions regarding the order of liquid/dry ingredients and set your machine to the dough/pizza setting.

To make the dough by hand

Place the flour and salt into a mixing bowl and mix together the yeast, sugar and water in a measuring jug. Pour the liquid into the dry ingredients and using your hands, mix together until it forms a dough and comes away from the bowl – it should take about 3–4 minutes. Transfer the dough onto a lightly floured work surface and knead (see basic instructions on page 27) for about 5–10 minutes. Return the dough back to the bowl, cover with cling film and leave in a warm place for 30–40 minutes to double in size. Scoop the bread back out and give it a simple knead for 1 minute.

To finish

Turn the dough onto a lightly floured surface and cut into eight pieces. Roll out each portion into a circle about 10cm (4in) in diameter. Lay a strip of greaseproof paper over one side of each of the circles and fold the dough over the paper to make a semi-circle. Place the folded flatbreads on a parchment-lined baking tray, cover and leave to prove for 20 minutes. Meanwhile, preheat the oven to 180°C (350°F), gas mark 4.

Bake the flatbreads in the preheated oven for 20 minutes until golden brown. To serve, fill the flatbreads with roasted pumpkin slices, mozzarella and salad leaves or air-dried ham, capers and rocket leaves dressed with olive oil and a little lemon juice – two great combinations.

Cumbrian whigg bread

I first tasted whigg bread as a young boy at a café in Hawkshead in the Lake District, which has since closed down. It's a delicious milk bread and is beautiful served with a top-quality strawberry or raspberry jam.

INGREDIENTS

500g (1lb) strong white bread flour

1¼ tsp salt

1 tsp fast-action/easy-blend yeast

1½ tsp granulated sugar

350ml (12fl oz) milk

1 tbsp caraway seeds

Here's how... To bake in a breadmaker

Place all of the ingredients into the bread pan following the manufacturers' instructions regarding the order of liquid/dry ingredients and set your machine to the basic/normal setting, large loaf, medium crust.

To bake by hand

Place the flour and salt into a mixing bowl and mix together the yeast, sugar, milk and caraway seeds in a measuring jug. Pour the liquid into the dry ingredients and using your hands, mix together until it forms a dough and comes away from the bowl – it should take about 3–4 minutes. Transfer the dough onto a lightly floured work surface and knead (see basic instructions on page 27) for about 5–10 minutes. Return the dough back to the bowl, cover with cling film and leave in a warm place for 30–40 minutes to double in size. Scoop the bread back out and give it a simple knead for 1 minute.

Shape the bread dough and place it in a 1kg (2lb) non-stick loaf tin and leave to prove for 30 minutes or until it has almost doubled in size. Meanwhile, preheat the oven to 200°C (400°F), gas mark 6.

Bake the bread in the preheated oven for 30–40 minutes until it is golden on top. To check if it is cooked, carefully slide the loaf out of the tin and tap the underneath. If it sounds hollow it is cooked, if not, return it to the oven for another 10 minutes.

Cider apple bread

An English classic, packed with distinctive flavours. Brilliant for making thick-cut sandwiches stuffed with almost any filling you can think of. It's also great with cheese.

INGREDIENTS

- 300g (10oz) strong white bread flour
- 200g (7oz) malted or granary-type flour
- 1 tsp salt
- 1 tsp ground white pepper
- 1 tsp fast-action/easy-blend yeast
- 1 tsp granulated sugar
- 350ml (12fl oz) dry cider
- 1 apple, grated
- 1 sprig fresh rosemary, chopped

Here's how... To bake in a breadmaker

Place all of the ingredients into the bread pan following the manufacturers' instructions regarding the order of liquid/dry ingredients and set your machine to the basic/normal setting, large loaf, medium crust.

To bake by hand

Place the two flours, salt and white pepper in a large mixing bowl. Mix together the yeast, sugar, cider, grated apple and rosemary in a measuring jug. Pour the liquid into the dry ingredients and using your hands, mix together until it forms a dough and comes away from the bowl – it should take about 3–4 minutes. Transfer the dough onto a lightly floured work surface and knead (see basic instructions on page 27) for about 5–10 minutes. Return the dough back to the bowl, cover with cling film and leave in a warm place for 30–40 minutes to double in size. Scoop the bread back out and give it a simple knead for 1 minute.

Transfer the smooth kneaded dough to a 1kg (2lb) non-stick loaf tin and leave somewhere warm to prove for 30–40 minutes or until almost doubled in size. Meanwhile, preheat the oven to 200°C (400°F), gas mark 6.

Bake the loaf in the preheated oven for 40 minutes until it is golden on top. To check if it is cooked, carefully slide the loaf out of the tin and tap the underneath. If it sounds hollow it is cooked, if not, return it to the oven for another 10 minutes.

Chestnut flour bread

I discovered chestnut flour on my travels through Italy. It gives bread a delicious smoky flavour and is also low in gluten. I have enjoyed it many times at a Tuscan market. You can make your own chestnut flour by whizzing roasted chestnuts in a food processor or blender.

INGREDIENTS

250g (8oz) strong white bread flour

250g (8oz) chestnut flour

1 tsp salt

1 tsp fast-action/easy-blend yeast

1 tsp granulated sugar

375ml (13fl oz) water

75g (3oz) sultanas

Here's how...To bake in a breadmaker

Place all of the ingredients, except the sultanas, into the bread pan following your manufacturers' instructions regarding the order of liquid/ dry ingredients. Place the sultanas in the nut/raisin dispenser (if available) and set your machine to the basic/normal raisin setting, large loaf, medium crust. If you do not have a nut/raisin dispenser, when the machine indicates (with a beeping sound) add the sultanas and close the lid.

To bake by hand

Place the two flours and salt into a mixing bowl and mix together the yeast, sugar, water and sultanas in a measuring jug. Pour the liquid into the dry ingredients and using your hands, mix together until it forms a dough and comes away from the bowl – it should take about 3–4 minutes. Transfer the dough onto a lightly floured work surface and knead (see basic instructions on page 27) for about 5–10 minutes. Return the dough back to the bowl, cover with cling film and leave in a warm place for 30–40 minutes to double in size. Scoop the bread back out and give it a simple knead for 1 minute.

Shape the dough into a round pizza shape about 2–3cm (½–1in) deep and transfer to a parchment-lined baking tray. Using kitchen scissors or a sharp knife, score the top of the dough and leave it to prove for about 30 minutes or until it doubles in size. Meanwhile, preheat the oven to 200°C (400°F), gas mark 6.

Bake the bread in the preheated oven for about 25–30 minutes until it is golden on top and sounds hollow when tapped underneath.

Coriander & cumin bread

These two spices are the backbone of aromatic Italian cooking and they make a truly tasty bread. Serve it with coronation chicken, invented in 1953 to celebrate Elizabeth II ascending the throne – the flavours go together beautifully.

INGREDIENTS

500g (1lb) strong white bread flour

1¼ tsp salt

1 tsp fast-action/easy-blend yeast

1½ tsp granulated sugar

350ml (12fl oz) water

25g (1oz) yogurt

1 tbsp cumin seeds, toasted

1 tbsp coriander seeds, toasted

Here's how... To bake in a breadmaker

Place all of the ingredients into the bread pan following the manufacturers' instructions regarding the order of liquid/dry ingredients and set your machine to the basic/normal setting, large loaf, medium crust.

To bake by hand

Place the flour and salt into a mixing bowl and mix together the yeast, sugar, water, yogurt and toasted seeds in a measuring jug. Pour the liquid into the dry ingredients and using your hands, mix together until it forms a dough and comes away from the bowl – it should take about 3–4 minutes. Transfer the dough onto a lightly floured work surface and knead (see basic instructions on page 27) for about 5–10 minutes. Return the dough back to the bowl, cover with cling film and leave in a warm place for 30–40 minutes to double in size. Scoop the bread back out and give it a simple knead for 1 minute.

Mould the bread dough into your desired shape, place on a non-stick baking tray and leave to prove for 30 minutes or until it has almost doubled in size. Meanwhile, preheat the oven to 200°C (400°F), gas mark 6.

Bake the bread in the preheated oven for 30–40 minutes until it is golden on top and sounds hollow when tapped underneath.

Chapter Three
Entertaining

Share with friends

I love entertaining at home. What could be more
exciting than sharing food with friends? I've never
met anyone who doesn't love freshly baked bread so
I always serve it at a dinner party or special occasion.
It's great to tear and share or to plunge into dips or
soups. Use spices, herbs and flavoured oils to turn
everyday breads into mouth-watering bites.

Worried about slaving over dough whilst your guests are knocking
at the door? Relax. Set your breadmaker to do all the hard work
before they arrive.

Every dinner party needs an ice-breaker. Sometimes, the
intoxicating aroma of freshly baked bread is enough to get everyone
talking before your guests have even taken off their coats.

I love it when friends invade the kitchen, drawn by the irresistible
smell of a warm loaf. If you really want to impress your guests cook
flatbreads in front of them, pour the wine and let the chatter and
laughter flow.

Pumpkin, walnut & blue cheese bread

Autumn is the season for pumpkins, but you can always substitute with roasted butternut squash at other times of the year. Tasty and crunchy, this bread is great torn into chunks and served with a hearty soup.

INGREDIENTS

100g (3½oz) pumpkin

1 tsp olive oil, plus a little extra for roasting

300ml (½ pint) water

1 tsp fast-action/easy-blend yeast

1 tsp granulated sugar

500g (1lb) strong white bread flour

1 tsp salt

¼ tsp ground white pepper

50g (2oz) good local blue cheese

50g (2oz) toasted walnuts

Salt and freshly ground black pepper

Here's how...

Preheat the oven to 200°C (400°F), gas mark 6.

First, roast the pumpkin. Cut it into quarters or eighths, season with salt and pepper and rub a little olive oil into the pumpkin flesh. Place it on a baking tray and roast in the preheated oven for 30 minutes or until the flesh is tender. When it is cool enough to handle, peel or cut the skin away and mash the sweet orange flesh with a fork or blend in a food processor until smooth.

To bake in a breadmaker

Place all the remaining ingredients, except the toasted walnuts, with the mashed pumpkin into the bread pan by following your manufacturers' instructions regarding the order of liquid/dry ingredients. Place the walnuts in the nut/raisin dispenser (if available) and set your machine to the basic/normal raisin setting, large loaf, medium crust. If you do not have a nut/raisin dispenser, when the machine indicates (with a beeping sound), add the toasted walnuts and close the lid.

To bake by hand

Place the water, yeast, sugar, 1 teaspoon oil and pumpkin purée into a large mixing bowl. Add the flour, salt, white pepper, blue cheese and walnuts. Using your hands, mix together until it forms a dough and comes away from the bowl – it should take about 3–4 minutes. Transfer the dough onto a lightly floured work surface and knead (see basic instructions on page 27) for about 5–10 minutes. Return the dough back to the bowl, cover with cling film and leave in a warm place for 30–40 minutes to double in size. Scoop the bread back out and give it a simple knead for 1 minute.

Transfer the dough to a 1kg (2lb) non-stick loaf tin and leave it somewhere warm to prove for 30–40 minutes or until it has almost doubled in size. Meanwhile, preheat the oven to 200°C (400°F), gas mark 6.

Bake the loaf in the preheated oven for 40 minutes until it is golden on top. To check if it is cooked, carefully slide the loaf out of the tin and tap the underneath. If it sounds hollow it is cooked, if not, return it to the oven for another 10 minutes.

Sesame & prawn bagel

A delicious bagel inspired by Chinese takeaway sesame prawn toast, which everyone seems to love. Serve with coriander, sliced spring onions, cucumber and sweet chilli dipping sauce.

INGREDIENTS

For the bagels

1 tsp fast-action/easy-blend yeast

400g (13oz) strong white bread flour

1 tbsp granulated sugar

¾ tsp salt

1 tbsp vegetable oil

250ml (8fl oz) water

1 egg yolk (optional)

For the topping

200g (7oz) raw tiger prawns, peeled

2 egg yolks

1 tsp Chinese five spice

2 tbsp double cream

4 tbsp sesame seeds

Here's how... To make the dough in a breadmaker

Place all of the bagel ingredients, except the egg yolk, into the bread pan following your manufacturers' instructions regarding the order of liquid/dry ingredients and set the machine to the dough/pizza setting. When the cycle is complete, remove the dough from the machine. Give it a simple knead for 1 minute, cover and allow the dough to rest for 10 minutes.

To make the dough by hand

Place the bagel ingredients, except the egg yolk, in a large mixing bowl. Use one hand to mix together until it forms a dough. Transfer the dough onto a lightly floured work surface and knead (see basic instructions on page 27) for about 5–10 minutes. Return the dough back to the bowl, cover with cling film and leave in a warm place for 30–40 minutes to double in size.

To finish

Divide the dough into nine equal portions. Working quickly, shape each into a smooth ball. Punch a hole in the centre and pull gently to produce a 5cm (2in) hole. Place them on a large greased baking sheet. Cover and leave to prove for 20 minutes (start timing after the first bagel is shaped).

Preheat the oven to 180°C (350°F), gas mark 4 and line a baking tray with non-stick baking parchment.

Bring a large shallow pan of water to the boil and place 3–4 bagels in at a time. Cook for 1–2 minutes on each side, then transfer them to the lined baking tray. Brush with an egg yolk wash, if desired, and bake in the preheated oven for 20 minutes until they are golden on top and sound hollow when tapped underneath.

While the bagels are baking remove the tails from the prawns and place them in a food processor. Blend with the egg yolks, five spice and cream until you have a thick paste-like consistency.

Remove the bagels from the oven and lower the oven temperature to 160°C (325°F), gas mark 3. Cut the bagels in half and spread the prawn mixture onto the cut side. Dip the bagel prawn-side down into the sesame seeds and place them back onto the baking tray. Return the bagels to the oven for 8–10 minutes to ensure the prawn mixture is cooked through. To check if the prawn mixture is cooked, press lightly. If firm to touch, they are done.

Herby flatbread

This recipe reminds me of the day my wife Emma and I moved into our first home, which did not even have a kitchen or oven. That night I just lit a barbecue, threw on some flatbreads, whipped up a pot of tzatziki and cracked open a few chilled beers. The unpacking had to wait.

INGREDIENTS

For the dough

500g (1lb) strong white bread flour

1¼ tsp salt

1 tsp fresh herbs e.g. rosemary, thyme, parsley or chives

1 tsp fast-action/easy-blend yeast

1½ tsp granulated sugar

300ml (½ pint) water

25ml (1fl oz) olive oil

For the tzatziki

1 x 300g (10oz) tub good-quality Greek yogurt

1 tsp dried mint

25ml (1fl oz) extra virgin olive oil

2 tbsp fresh mint, finely chopped

½ garlic clove, crushed

Salt and freshly ground black pepper

Here's how... To make the dough in a breadmaker

Place all of the dough ingredients into the bread pan following the manufacturers' instructions regarding the order of liquid/dry ingredients and set your machine to the dough/pizza setting.

To make the dough by hand

Place the flour, salt and fresh herbs into a mixing bowl and mix together the yeast, sugar, water and oil in a measuring jug. Pour the liquid into the dry ingredients and using your hands, mix together until it forms a dough and comes away from the bowl – it should take about 3–4 minutes. Transfer the dough onto a lightly floured work surface and knead (see basic instructions on page 27) for about 5–10 minutes. Return the dough back to the bowl, cover with cling film and leave in a warm place for 30–40 minutes to double in size.

To finish

Whilst the dough is being made, make the tzatziki: place the yogurt in a bowl and add the dried mint and olive oil. Add the fresh mint and garlic to the bowl and mix well. Season to taste and refrigerate until needed.

Place the dough on a lightly floured work surface. Knead for about a minute then cut the dough into 10 pieces. Roll each piece out flat, about 1cm (½in) thick, and lay them on a plate; place a piece of baking parchment between each flatbread to keep them separated.

The flatbreads can be cooked either in a frying pan or on a barbecue grill – simply heat a dry frying pan and cook the breads for about 1–2 minutes on each side. When using a barbecue, choose the coolest place on the grill (usually at the sides) and cook the flatbreads for 1–2 minutes on each side. Serve with the chilled tzatziki.

Walnut & rosemary focaccia

I've been making focaccia for a long time now, but you're never too young to learn a new trick or two. I was taught this way of making focaccia by a 16-year-old lad from Tuscany. Adding mashed potato to the bread seems to add a richness that works really well with the olive oil.

INGREDIENTS

3 tbsp walnuts

1 tbsp vegetable oil

250g (8oz) strong white bread flour

200g (7oz) 00 Italian pasta flour

1 heaped tsp of salt

1 cooked jacket potato

1 tsp of fast-action/easy-blend yeast

300ml (½ pint) water

25ml (1fl oz) extra virgin olive oil

1 tbsp rosemary leaves

1 tsp coarse sea salt

Here's how...

Place the walnuts into a dry frying pan over a medium heat with the vegetable oil. Cook the walnuts for a few minutes until golden and crunchy. Remove from the heat and allow to cool.

To make the dough in the breadmaker

Place both the flours into the bread pan with the salt. Cut the cooked jacket potato in half and scoop out the inside into a measuring jug. Using a spoon, mash the potato until smooth. Add the yeast and water to the mashed potato and mix until it all dissolves. Pour this into the bread pan. Add the roasted walnuts and set your machine to the dough only setting.

To make the dough by hand

Place both the flours and the salt in a large mixing bowl. Cut the cooked jacket potato in half and scoop out the inside into a measuring jug. Using a spoon, mash the potato until smooth. Add the yeast and water to the mashed potato and mix until it all dissolves. Add this to the flour and salt and using your hands, mix together until it forms a dough and comes away from the bowl – it should take about 3–4 minutes. Transfer the dough to a lightly floured work surface and knead (see basic instructions on page 27) for about 5–10 minutes. Flatten out the dough and scatter the roasted walnuts all over. Continue to knead for 1 minute to mix in the nuts. Place the dough back into the bowl, cover with cling film and leave in a warm place for 30–40 minutes or until it has almost doubled in size.

To finish

Preheat the oven to 220°C (425°F), gas mark 7. Turn out or transfer the dough onto a very lightly floured work surface, roll it out into a round pizza base shape – it should be about 2.5–5cm (1–2in) thick and place on a non-stick baking tray. Using clean hands, use your finger to push little holes all over the dough and drizzle with plenty of extra virgin olive oil – the oil should dribble into the holes you have made to create wells of richness.

Scatter over the rosemary leaves and sea salt and bake for 20 minutes or until the bread is golden and sounds hollow when tapped underneath. Remove the bread from the oven and give the bread a final drizzle of olive oil to reinforce that great peppery olive flavour.

Breadsticks

Shop-bought breadsticks are often dry and tasteless. These are fun to make and absolutely delicious – you'll never go back to shop-bought breadsticks again.

INGREDIENTS

500g (1lb) strong white bread flour

1 tsp salt

1 tsp fast-action/easy-blend yeast

1 tsp granulated sugar

275ml (9fl oz) water

1 beaten egg

For the fillings

Olive tapenade and Parmesan

Pesto

Sea salt and rosemary

Dijon mustard and Cheddar

Here's how...To make the dough in a breadmaker

Place all of the dough ingredients, except the beaten egg, into the bread pan following the manufacturers' instructions regarding the order of liquid/dry ingredients and set your machine to the dough/pizza setting.

To make the dough by hand

Place the flour and salt into a mixing bowl and mix together the yeast, sugar and water in a measuring jug. Pour the liquid into the dry ingredients and using your hands, mix together until it forms a dough and comes away from the bowl – it should take about 3–4 minutes. Transfer the dough onto a lightly floured work surface and knead (see basic instructions on page 27) for about 5–10 minutes. Return the dough back to the bowl, cover with cling film and leave in a warm place for 30–40 minutes to double in size. Scoop the bread back out and give it a simple knead for 1 minute.

To finish

Preheat the oven to 180°C (350°F), gas mark 4 and line a baking tray with non-stick baking parchment.

Turn the dough out onto a lightly floured work surface and divide into two. Roll out the first portion into a rectangle about 5mm (¼in) thick. Top one half of the dough with your chosen filling and fold over to encase the contents. Roll the filled dough back into the original rectangle shape and cut into strips about 2cm (¾in) wide. Place on the lined baking tray.

Repeat with the second portion of dough. Experiment with different fillings and by twisting the dough sticks before baking.

Brush the breadsticks with the beaten egg and bake in the preheated oven for about 20 minutes until golden brown and crisp.

Naan with cumin & black onion seeds

I was brought up in Yorkshire and a 'lads' night out' usually involved a curry, lots of naan breads to mop up the juices and a few beers. Life has moved on and most of us are now married with young kids, so this recipe – served with a spicy balti or dansak – is perfect for a 'lads' night in' and a few less beers.

INGREDIENTS

1 tsp cumin seeds

1 tsp black onion seeds

500g (1lb) strong white bread flour

1 tsp salt

1 tsp fast-action/easy-blend yeast

1 tsp granulated sugar

50ml (2fl oz) yogurt

275ml (9fl oz) water

Here's how...

Toast the seeds in a dry frying pan until they start to crackle.

To make the dough in a breadmaker

Place all of the ingredients into the bread pan following the manufacturers' instructions regarding the order of liquid/dry ingredients, add the toasted seeds and set your machine to the dough/pizza setting.

To make the dough by hand

Place the flour and salt into a mixing bowl and mix together the yeast, sugar, yogurt, water and toasted seeds in a measuring jug. Pour the liquid into the dry ingredients and using your hands, mix together until it forms a dough and comes away from the bowl – it should take about 3–4 minutes. Transfer the dough onto a lightly floured work surface and knead (see basic instructions on page 27) for about 5–10 minutes. Return the dough back to the bowl, cover with cling film and leave in a warm place for 30–40 minutes to double in size.

To finish

Preheat the oven to 200°C (400°F), gas mark 6 and preheat one or two baking trays.

Turn the dough out onto a lightly floured work surface and knead the bread by hand for about a minute. Cut the dough into six portions and roll each portion into an oval shape about 1cm (½in) thick.

Place the naan on the hot baking tray(s) and cook in the preheated oven for about 10 minutes. Alternatively, cook the naan in a dry frying pan over a low heat for 3–4 minutes on each side until golden and cooked through.

Ciabatta with black olives

Ciabatta is often served with a good pasta dish but I prefer to just dip it into a high-quality virgin olive oil or equally tasty balsamic vinegar.

INGREDIENTS

For the starter dough (see page 17)

1 tsp fast-action/easy-blend yeast

500g (1lb) strong white bread flour

475ml (16fl oz) water

For the ciabatta

500g (1lb) starter dough

250g (8oz) strong white bread flour, plus extra for dusting and kneading

40ml (1½fl oz) water

1½ tsp salt

1 tsp fast-action/easy-blend yeast

50ml (2fl oz) extra virgin olive oil

100g (3½oz) pitted black olives, chopped

Here's how...

For the starter dough, mix the ingredients in a bowl, cover with a clean tea towel and secure with an elastic band. Leave for 12 hours to prove at room temperature.

To make the dough in a breadmaker

Place the proved starter dough into the bread pan and follow the manufacturers' instructions regarding the order of the remaining liquid/dry ingredients (but using just half the olive oil and omitting the olives at this stage). Set your machine to the dough/pizza setting.

To make the dough by hand

Place the starter dough and the remaining ingredients in a large mixing bowl (but only use half the olive oil and omit the olives at this stage). Using your hands, mix together until it forms a dough and comes away from the bowl – it should take about 3–4 minutes. Transfer the dough onto a lightly floured work surface and knead (see basic instructions on page 27) for about 5–10 minutes. Return the dough back to the bowl, cover with cling film and leave in a warm place for 30–40 minutes to double in size. Scoop the bread back out and give it a simple knead for 1 minute.

To finish

Turn the dough out onto a lightly floured surface and knead in the black olives. Place the dough in a shallow dish and drizzle over the remaining olive oil. Cover and leave in a warm to prove for 3 hours.

Preheat the oven to 230°C (450°F), gas mark 8. Place the ciabatta on a non-stick baking tray or preheated bread stone and transfer to the preheated oven. Reduce the temperature to 200°C (400°F), gas mark 6 and bake for 30–40 minutes until it is golden on top and sounds hollow when tapped underneath.

Fennel & sultana bread

I love the combination of sultanas and fennel. The aniseed flavour of the fennel is perfectly offset by the sweetness of the dried fruit. This recipe also includes a little rye flour to give it an even richer flavour.

INGREDIENTS

For the starter dough (See page 17)

1 tsp fast-action/easy-blend yeast

500g (1lb) strong white bread flour

475ml (16fl oz) water

For the dough

500g (1lb) starter dough

250g (8oz) dark rye flour

1½ tsp salt

1 tsp fast-action/easy-blend yeast

1 tsp granulated sugar

100ml (3½fl oz) water

2 tsp fennel seeds

75g (3oz) plump sultanas

Here's how...

For the starter dough, mix the ingredients in a bowl, cover with a clean tea towel and secure with an elastic band. Leave for 12 hours to prove at room temperature.

To bake in a breadmaker

Place all of the dough ingredients, except the fennel seeds and sultanas, together with the starter dough into the bread pan following your manufacturers' instructions regarding the order of liquid/dry ingredients. Place the fennel seeds and sultanas in the nut/raisin dispenser (if available) and set your machine to the basic/normal raisin setting, large loaf, medium crust. If you do not have a nut/raisin dispenser, when the machine indicates (with a beeping sound), add the fennel seeds and sultanas and close the lid.

To bake by hand

Place the starter dough, rye flour and salt into a mixing bowl and mix together the yeast, sugar, water, fennel seeds and sultanas in a measuring jug. Pour the liquid into the dry ingredients and using your hands, mix together until it forms a dough and comes away from the bowl – it should take about 3–4 minutes. Transfer the dough onto a lightly floured work surface and knead (see basic instructions on page 27) for about 5–10 minutes. Return the dough back to the bowl, cover with cling film and leave in a warm place for 30–40 minutes to double in size. Scoop the bread back out and give it a simple knead for 1 minute.

Shape the dough into a large ring, place it on a non-stick baking tray and leave the dough to prove for about 30 minutes or until it doubles in size. Preheat the oven to 200°C (400°F), gas mark 6.

Bake the bread in the preheated oven for about 25–30 minutes or until it is golden on top and sounds hollow when tapped underneath.

Sun-dried tomato & thyme loaf

Sun-dried tomatoes add an intense flavour to any dish and this bread recipe is no exception. It is delicious with almost any Mediterranean dish but I especially like to enjoy it toasted and spread with pesto.

INGREDIENTS

500g (1lb) strong white bread flour

1¼ tsp salt

1 tsp fast-action/easy-blend yeast

1½ tsp granulated sugar

350ml (12fl oz) water (including 100ml (3½fl oz) water from the soaked sun-dried tomatoes)

2 tsp fresh thyme, chopped

12 sun-dried tomatoes, soaked in water and chopped

Here's how... To bake in a breadmaker

Place all of the dough ingredients, except the sun-dried tomatoes, into the bread pan following your manufacturers' instructions regarding the order of dry/liquid ingredients. Place the sun-dried tomatoes in the nut/raisin dispenser (if available) and set your machine to the basic/normal raisin setting, large loaf, light crust. If you do not have a nut/raisin dispenser, when the machine indicates (with a beeping sound) add the sun-dried tomatoes and close the lid.

To bake by hand

Place the flour and salt in a large mixing bowl and mix together the yeast, sugar, water, and thyme in a measuring jug. Pour the liquid into the dry ingredients and using your hands, mix together until it forms a dough and comes away from the bowl – it should take about 3–4 minutes. Transfer the dough onto a lightly floured work surface and knead (see basic instructions on page 27) for about 5–10 minutes. Return the dough back to the bowl, cover with cling film and leave in a warm place for 30–40 minutes to double in size. Scoop the bread back out and give it a simple knead for 1 minute.

Shape the dough into a round loaf and place it on a non-stick baking tray. Leave it somewhere warm to prove for 30–40 minutes or until it has almost doubled in size. Preheat the oven to 200°C (400°F), gas mark 6.

Bake the loaf in the preheated oven for 40 minutes until it is golden on top and sounds hollow when tapped underneath.

Sweet potato & smoked paprika bread

This is a warming bread and a great favourite with my customers – especially those who have just spent several hours on a wintry fell in the Lake District! It goes down a storm served with tomato and goat's cheese soup or a thick wintry stew.

INGREDIENTS

200g (7oz) sweet potatoes

500g (1lb) strong white bread flour

1 tsp salt

1 tsp fast-action/easy-blend yeast

1 tsp granulated sugar

300ml (½ pint) water

1 tbsp smoked sweet paprika

Here's how...

Preheat the oven to 190°C (375°F), gas mark 5 and bake the sweet potatoes for about 30–40 minutes until soft. Remove the skins and mash well. Set aside until needed.

To bake in a breadmaker

Place all of the ingredients into the bread pan following the manufacturers' instructions regarding the order of liquid/dry ingredients and add the mashed sweet potato and paprika. Set your machine to the basic/normal setting, large loaf, medium crust.

To bake by hand

Place the flour and salt into a large mixing bowl and mix together the yeast, sugar, water and paprika in a measuring jug. Pour the liquid into the dry ingredients, add the mashed sweet potato and using your hands, mix together until it forms a dough and comes away from the bowl – it should take about 3–4 minutes. Transfer the dough onto a lightly floured work surface and knead (see basic instructions on page 27) for about 5–10 minutes. Return the dough back to the bowl, cover with cling film and leave in a warm place for 30–40 minutes to double in size. Scoop the bread back out and give it a simple knead for 1 minute.

Transfer the dough to a 1kg (2lb) non-stick loaf tin and leave it somewhere warm to prove for 30–40 minutes or until almost doubled in size. Preheat the oven to 200°C (400°F), gas mark 6.

Bake the loaf in the preheated oven for 40 minutes until golden on top. To check if it is cooked, carefully slide the loaf out of the tin and tap the underneath. If it sounds hollow it is cooked, if not, return it to the oven for another 10 minutes.

Chorizo & blackened chilli bread

Tapas platters have never been more popular, probably part of the trend towards more informal ways of eating and socialising. Your friends will fight for a chunk of this sharp-tasting bread, so make enough to go round.

INGREDIENTS

1 red chilli

500g (1lb) strong white bread flour

1¼ tsp salt

1 tsp fast-action/easy-blend yeast

1½ tsp granulated sugar

300ml (½ pint) water

25ml (1fl oz) olive oil

100g (3½oz) chorizo, diced

Here's how...

Blacken the chilli by placing it in aluminium foil and burning it in a flame from a gas hob or by frying in oil in a frying pan. When the chilli is cool, remove the blackened skin and deseed if you prefer, or leave it all as is and dice it as finely as possible.

To bake in a breadmaker

Place all of the dough ingredients, except the chorizo, with the blackened chilli into the bread pan following your manufacturers' instructions regarding the order of liquid/dry ingredients. Place the chorizo in the nut/raisin dispenser (if available) and set your machine to the basic/normal raisin setting, large loaf, medium crust. If you do not have a nut/raisin dispenser, when the machine indicates (with a beeping sound), add the chorizo and close the lid.

To bake by hand

Place the flour and salt in a large mixing bowl and mix together the yeast, sugar, water, oil, blackened chilli and chorizo in a measuring jug. Pour the liquid into the dry ingredients and using your hands, mix together until it forms a dough and comes away from the bowl – it should take about 3–4 minutes. Transfer the dough onto a lightly floured work surface and knead (see basic instructions on page 27) for about 5–10 minutes. Return the dough back to the bowl, cover with cling film and leave in a warm place for 30–40 minutes to double in size. Scoop the bread back out and give it a simple knead for 1 minute.

Mould the dough into a long oval bloomer shape and place it on a non-stick baking tray. Cover and leave in a warm place to prove for 30–40 minutes or until it has almost doubled in size. Meanwhile, preheat the oven to 200°C (400°F), gas mark 6.

Bake the loaf in the preheated oven for 40 minutes until it is golden on top and sounds hollow when tapped underneath.

Mustard & tarragon swirl

This is a fantastic savoury bread. Instead of one large loaf, try baking small rolls inside new, clean terracotta pots – yes, the same ones you buy from the garden centre – it really works.

INGREDIENTS

500g (1lb) strong white bread flour

1¼ tsp salt

1 tsp fast-action/easy-blend yeast

1½ tsp granulated sugar

300ml (½ pint) water

For the flavouring

3 tbsp Dijon mustard

1 tsp fresh tarragon, chopped

1 egg yolk, beaten

1 tsp mustard seeds (optional)

1 tsp sea salt (optional)

Here's how... To make the dough in a breadmaker

Place all of the dough ingredients into the bread pan following the manufacturers' instructions regarding the order of liquid/dry ingredients and set your machine to the dough/pizza setting.

To make the dough by hand

Place the flour and salt in a large mixing bowl and mix together the yeast, sugar and water in a measuring jug. Pour the liquid into the dry ingredients and using your hands, mix together until it forms a dough and comes away from the bowl – it should take about 3–4 minutes. Transfer the dough onto a lightly floured work surface and knead (see basic instructions on page 27) for about 5–10 minutes. Return the dough back to the bowl, cover with cling film and leave in a warm place for 30–40 minutes to double in size. Scoop the bread back out and give it a simple knead for 1 minute.

To finish

Roll the dough into 12 small sausage shapes. Using a pastry brush, spread the mustard along the lengths of the dough, sprinkle with chopped tarragon, shape each dough sausage into a coil and transfer them to 12 small terracotta pots. Brush with the beaten egg yolk and sprinkle with mustard seeds and a little sea salt, if desired. Alternatively, leave the dough in one piece and roll it into one big sausage shape and continue to add the flavouring as above. Put the dough on a non-stick baking tray.

Leave the bread to prove for an hour or until it doubles in size. Meanwhile, preheat the oven to 200°C (400°F), gas mark 6.

Bake the bread for 15–20 minutes if using the small terracotta pots and 45 minutes if baking it whole, until it is golden on top. To check if it is cooked, carefully slide the loaves out of the pots and tap the underneath. If it sounds hollow it is cooked, if not, return it to the oven for another 10 minutes.

Mozzarella & cherry tomato loaf

For this loaf I've simply used the ingredients from one of the most popular starters in Italian restaurants throughout the land. It makes a great dipping bread.

INGREDIENTS

10 cherry tomatoes, halved

1 mozzarella ball, sliced

1 handful of fresh basil leaves

For the dough

500g (1lb) strong white bread flour

1¼ tsp salt

1 tsp fast-action/easy-blend yeast

1½ tsp granulated sugar

300ml (½ pint) water

25ml (1fl oz) olive oil

Here's how... To make the dough in a breadmaker

Place all of the dough ingredients into the bread pan following the manufacturers' instructions regarding the order of liquid/dry ingredients and set your machine to the dough/pizza setting.

To make the dough by hand

Place the flour and salt in a large mixing bowl and mix together the yeast, sugar, water and oil in a measuring jug. Pour the liquid into the dry ingredients and using your hands, mix together until it forms a dough and comes away from the bowl – it should take about 3–4 minutes. Transfer the dough onto a lightly floured work surface and knead (see basic instructions on page 27) for about 5–10 minutes. Return the dough back to the bowl, cover with cling film and leave in a warm place for 30–40 minutes to double in size. Scoop the bread back out and give it a simple knead for 1 minute.

To finish

Roll the dough out to a rectangle about 40 x 20cm (16 x 8in). Scatter the halved cherry tomatoes and mozzarella over the centre third of the dough. Tear up the basil leaves and sprinkle them on top of the tomatoes and mozzarella. Using a sharp knife make 5cm (2in) long cuts into the dough about 2.5cm (1in) wide all the way along one outside edge of dough, then do the same on the other side. Now, take the first cut on the right and fold it over the middle to cover the filling, then do the same from the left. Continue to do this on alternate sides until the filling is covered and you have a very pretty plaited bread loaf.

Carefully transfer to a lined baking tray and leave to prove in a warm place for about 40 minutes or until it doubles in size. Preheat the oven to 200°C (400°F), gas mark 6.

Bake in the preheated oven about for 30 minutes until it is golden on top and sounds hollow when tapped underneath.

Goat's cheese & roasted red pepper bread

Tear 'n' share breads are great for parties and summer buffets in the garden and this recipe is universally popular with my family and friends. Invariably, one tray is never enough.

INGREDIENTS

1 red pepper

100g (3½oz) goat's cheese, crumbled

1 beaten egg (yolk only)

For the dough

500g (1lb) strong white bread flour

1¼ tsp salt

1 tsp fast-action/easy-blend yeast

1½ tsp granulated sugar

300ml (½ pint) water

Here's how...

Preheat the oven to 200°C (400°F), gas mark 6 and cook the red pepper on a baking tray for 20 minutes until soft. Remove the pepper from the oven, put it into a plastic bag and seal (or put into a bowl and cover it with cling film) – this will cause the pepper to steam and separate the skin from the flesh. After 10 minutes remove the pepper from the bag, scrape off the skin and dice the flesh roughly into 1cm (½in) pieces. Set aside until needed.

To make the dough in a breadmaker

Place all of the dough ingredients into the bread pan following the manufacturers' instructions regarding the order of liquid/dry ingredients and set your machine to the dough/pizza setting.

To make the dough by hand

Place the flour and salt in a large mixing bowl and mix together the yeast, sugar and water in a measuring jug. Pour the liquid into the dry ingredients and using your hands, mix together until it forms a dough and comes away from the bowl – it should take about 3–4 minutes. Transfer the dough onto a lightly floured work surface and knead (see basic instructions on page 27) for about 5–10 minutes. Return the dough back to the bowl, cover with cling film and leave in a warm place for 30–40 minutes to double in size. Scoop the bread back out and give it a simple knead for 1 minute.

To finish

Turn the dough out on to a lightly floured work surface and roll it into a 40 x 30cm (16 x 12in) rectangle. Spread the surface of the dough evenly with the roasted red pepper and sprinkle with the goat's cheese. Roll the far side of the dough towards you to make a Swiss roll. Cut the dough into 2.5cm (1in) slices.

Line a 25cm (10in) cake tin with baking parchment and place the slices cut-side down into the tin. Brush with the egg yolk and leave to prove for 30–40 minutes. As the dough proves it will expand and link all the portions together. Preheat the oven to 220°C (425°F), gas mark 7.

Bake the bread for 20–25 minutes or until golden brown on top.

Chapter Four
Outdoor

Rye with pecans & millet seeds

Gingerbread

Malt loaf

Johnny cakes

Brazil nut wholemeal bread

Chelsea buns with super foods

Banana bread

Pressed focaccia

Eating alfresco

Bread, like all foods, tastes better outdoors – whether in the park with the kids, on top of a mountain, by a river with your mates or in the back garden with the neighbours. But there's a lot more to eating bread outside than simple sandwiches.

Baking a loaf of bread or a cake always seems like a great place to start when putting together a picnic for a nice alfresco meal. Bread can easily be the centrepiece to a great meal or it can even be the container – either way bread is magnificent and versatile and can be enjoyed whether you are under an umbrella or a parasol.

The Pressed focaccia bread on page 114 is perfect for enjoying outdoors and can be adapted to use any kind of compact loaf. I sometimes cook fresh pizzas topped with herbs from the garden in a wood oven outdoors – they are truly delicious.

Be inspired to try something different in your life – by trying a new outdoor activity and in your cooking. Great health and great bread go hand in hand.

Rye with pecans & millet seeds

This is a nutty-flavoured bread, full of energy, fibre and omega-3 oils to power you through the day. Great for athletes and the health-conscious.

INGREDIENTS

300g (10oz) rye flour

200g (7oz) granary flour

1 tsp salt

1 tsp fast-action/easy-blend yeast

1 tsp granulated sugar

375ml (13fl oz) water

For the roasted nuts & seeds

100g (3½oz) pecans

50g (2oz) millet seeds

1 tsp olive oil

Sea salt

Here's how...

Preheat the oven to 160°C (325°F), gas mark 3.

Roast the pecans and millet seeds by spreading them out onto a non-stick baking tray, season with a drizzle of olive oil and a little sea salt and cook in the preheated oven for 10–15 minutes until golden and crispy.

To bake in a breadmaker

Place all of the ingredients including the roasted nuts and seeds into the pan following your manufacturers' instructions regarding the order of liquid/dry ingredients and set your machine to the rye setting.

To bake by hand

Place both the flours, salt and the roasted nuts and seeds in a mixing bowl and mix together the yeast, sugar and water in a measuring jug. Pour the liquid into the dry ingredients and using your hands, mix together until it forms a dough and comes away from the bowl – it should take about 3–4 minutes. Transfer the dough onto a lightly floured work surface and knead (see basic instructions on page 27) for about 5–10 minutes. Return the dough back to the bowl, cover with cling film and leave in a warm place for 30–40 minutes to double in size. Scoop the bread back out and give it a simple knead for 1 minute.

Transfer the dough to a 1kg (2lb) non-stick loaf tin and leave somewhere warm to prove for 30–40 minutes or until it has almost doubled in size. Meanwhle, preheat the oven to 200°C (400°F), gas mark 6.

Bake the loaf in the preheated oven for 40 minutes until it is golden on top. To check if it is cooked, carefully slide the loaf out of the tin and tap the underneath. If it sounds hollow it is cooked, if not, return it to the oven for another 10 minutes.

Gingerbread

As a kid I loved ginger nut biscuits and this bread is a nostalgic nod to the past. Spicy, pungent and full of the feel-good factor, not to mention a great treat for picnics.

INGREDIENTS

100g (3½oz) muscovado sugar

75g (3oz) butter

75g (3oz) golden syrup

75g (3oz) black treacle

225g (7½oz) plain flour

1 tsp ground ginger

1½ tsp baking powder

1½ tsp bicarbonate of soda

½ tsp mixed spice

100ml (3½fl oz) ginger beer

50ml (2fl oz) full-fat milk

1 large egg, beaten

75g (3oz) candied ginger,
    chopped

Here's how...

Melt the sugar, butter, syrup and treacle in a saucepan over a low heat.

Sift together the flour, ground ginger, baking powder, bicarbonate of soda and the mixed spice into a large mixing bowl. Make a well in the middle of the flour and pour in the melted butter mixture from the saucepan.

Add the ginger beer, milk, egg and the candied ginger and mix well until smooth.

To bake in a breadmaker

Remove the paddle and line the bread pan up the sides with silicone baking parchment. Pour the mixture into the prepared pan and set the machine to the bake only setting for 50 minutes. Test the bread after about 40 minutes by pressing the top gently, if it springs back it is cooked. If not then it will need a little longer.

To bake by hand

Preheat the oven to 160°C (325°F), gas mark 3.

Pour the mixture into a 1kg (2lb) loaf tin lined with baking parchment and bake in the preheated oven for 40–50 minutes. Test the bread after about 40 minutes by pressing the top gently, if it springs back it is cooked. If not then it will need a little longer.

Malt loaf

Malt loaf is an iconic product and a great favourite with people on the coast-to-coast cycle route that passes through Keswick, near my bistro.

INGREDIENTS

1 tsp granulated sugar

75g (3oz) butter

1 tbsp molasses

1 tbsp black treacle

1 tbsp malt extract

200g (7oz) strong wholemeal bread flour

200g (7oz) strong white bread flour

1 tsp salt

250ml (8fl oz) water

1 tsp fast-action/easy-blend yeast

200g (7oz) sultanas

Here's how... To bake in a breadmaker

Place all of the ingredients into the bread pan, except the sultanas, following the manufacturers' instructions regarding the order of liquid/dry ingredients. Place the sultanas in the nut/raisin dispenser (if available) and set your machine to the wholewheat raisin setting, medium loaf, medium crust. If you do not have a nut/raisin dispenser, when the machine indicates (with a beeping sound), add the sultanas and close the lid.

To bake by hand

Preheat the oven to 160°C (325°F), gas mark 3 and line a 1kg (2lb) loaf tin with baking parchment.

In a saucepan over low heat to avoid burning, melt the sugar, butter, molasses, treacle and malt extract.

Place both flours and the salt in a large mixing bowl. Make a well in the centre and add the water, yeast and sultanas. Mix it all together until smooth. Stir in the melted butter mixture and mix together.

Pour the mixture into the prepared loaf tin and bake in the preheated oven for 40–50 minutes until the top is firm.

Johnny cakes

Also called Twisters and Dampers, this bread originates in the Australian outback. Every time I cook it outdoors passers-by stop to have a look and a taste. A true 'people's' bread.

INGREDIENTS

500g (1lb) self-raising flour, plus extra for shaping

1 tsp salt

1 tsp ground white pepper

8 sun-dried tomatoes, chopped

1 x 300ml (½ pint) bottle of beer

Here's how...

In a bowl mix together the flour, salt and pepper and chopped sun-dried tomatoes. Pour in the beer and bring the ingredients together to form a dough using your hands.

When the dough comes away from the bowl and is at a manageable consistency divide, it into 10–12 portions and shape into rounds or ovals with a little flour.

Check the barbecue and when it is glowing and white, place the Johnny cakes one at a time on the edge of the grill (the coolest part) for about 2–3 minutes on each side so they puff up and are crisp on the outside.

You can also turn them into 'twisters' by rolling out thin strips, wrapping them around a stick and cooking over an open fire for 2–3 minutes.

Alternatively, you can cook them in an oven preheated to 200°C (400°F), gas mark 6. Place the cakes on a non-stick baking tray and cook for 8–10 minutes until golden and cooked through.

Brazil nut wholemeal bread

Brazil nuts are really good for you and packed with goodness for an active lifestyle. Its not always easy to get nuts into your diet so this recipe works really well as the Brazil nuts give a great flavour and a real contrast in texture to the loaf.

INGREDIENTS

250g (8oz) strong white bread flour

200g (7oz) strong wholemeal bread flour

50g (2oz) muesli

1 tsp salt

1 tsp fast-action/easy-blend yeast

25ml (1fl oz) vegetable oil

25g (1oz) black treacle or molasses

180ml (6fl oz) water

180g (6oz) yogurt

For the roasted nuts

75g (3oz) chopped Brazil nuts

1 tsp olive oil

Salt

Here's how...

Preheat the oven to 150°C (300°F), gas mark 2. Roast the Brazil nuts by placing them on a dry roasting tray or ovenproof dish. Drizzle a little oil and sprinkle some salt over them and bake in the preheated oven for 10 minutes, until golden and crunchy.

To bake in a breadmaker

Place all of the ingredients into the bread pan, except the roasted Brazil nuts, by following your manufacturers' instructions regarding liquid/dry ingredients. Place the Brazil nuts in the nut/raisin dispenser (if available) and set your machine to the basic/normal raisin setting, large loaf, medium crust. If you do not have a nut/raisin dispenser, when the machine indicates (with a beeping sound), add the Brazil nuts and close the lid.

To bake by hand

Place both of the flours, muesli, salt and the roasted nuts in a mixing bowl and mix together the yeast, oil, treacle or molasses, water and yogurt in a measuring jug. Pour the liquid into the dry ingredients and using your hands, mix together until it forms a dough and comes away from the bowl – it should take about 3–4 minutes. Transfer the dough onto a lightly floured work surface and knead (see basic instructions on page 27) for about 5–10 minutes. Return the dough back to the bowl, cover with cling film and leave in a warm place for 30–40 minutes to double in size. Scoop the bread back out and give it a simple knead for 1 minute.

Transfer the dough to a 1kg (2lb) non-stick loaf tin and leave it somewhere warm to prove for 30–40 minutes, or until it has almost doubled in size. Meanwhile, preheat the oven to 200°C (400°F), gas mark 6.

Bake the loaf in the preheated oven for 40 minutes until it is golden on top. To check if it is cooked, carefully slide the loaf out of the tin and tap the underneath. If it sounds hollow it is cooked, if not, return it to the oven for another 10 minutes.

Chelsea buns with superfoods

This loaf might seem like you're having a naughty cake but you're actually getting lots of superfoods full of vitamins and antioxidants, which is always a good thing for an active day.

INGREDIENTS

500g (1lb) granary flour

1 tsp salt

1 tsp fast-action/easy-blend yeast

1 tsp granulated sugar

325ml (11fl oz) full-fat milk

Zest of 1 lemon

1 egg yolk, beaten

For the filling

100g (3½oz) dried sultanas

100g (3½oz) dried blueberries

100g (3½oz) dried cranberries

Juice of 1 lemon

100g (3½oz) granulated sugar

Here's how...

To make the filling, place the dried fruit into a bowl, squeeze the lemon juice over the top and leave it to soak while the dough is being prepared.

To make the dough in a breadmaker

Place all of the dough ingredients, except the egg yolk, in the bread pan following the manufacturers' instructions regarding the order of liquid/dry ingredients and set your machine to the pizza/dough setting.

To make the dough by hand

Place the flour and salt in a mixing bowl and mix together the yeast, sugar, milk and lemon zest in a measuring jug. Pour the liquid into the dry ingredients and using your hands, mix together until it forms a dough and comes away from the bowl – it should take about 3–4 minutes. Transfer the dough onto a lightly floured work surface and knead (see basic instructions on page 27) for about 5–10 minutes. Return the dough back to the bowl, cover with cling film and leave in a warm place for 30–40 minutes to double in size. Scoop the bread back out and give it a simple knead for 1 minute.

To finish

Turn the dough out onto a lightly floured work surface. Using a rolling pin, roll the dough into a 40 x 30cm (16 x 12in) rectangle. Spread evenly with the lemon-soaked dried fruit and sprinkle with sugar. Roll the far side of the dough towards you to make a Swiss roll. Cut the dough into 3cm (1in) slices.

Line a 25cm (10in) cake tin with baking parchment, place the slices cut-side down into the prepared tin, brush with the beaten egg yolk and leave it to prove for 30–40 minutes. As the dough proves it will expand and link all the portions together. Meanwhile, preheat the oven to 220°C (425°F), gas mark 7.

Bake the buns in the preheated oven for 20–25 minutes until golden.

Banana bread

Ripe bananas work best in this delicious bread that is incredibly moreish, packed with instant energy and perfect picnic food.

INGREDIENTS

100g (3½oz) butter

175g (6oz) caster sugar

2 large eggs, beaten

200g (7oz) self-raising flour, sifted

½ tsp baking powder

200g (7oz) ripe bananas

75g (3oz) yogurt

½ tsp nutmeg

125g (4oz) plump sultanas

100g (3½oz) roasted walnuts or pecans

50g (2oz) poppy seeds

Here's how...

In a bowl cream together the butter and the sugar until it is light and fluffy. Add the beaten eggs, then the flour and baking powder a little at a time until it is all incorporated.

Mash the bananas until smooth and stir into the mixture along with the yogurt. Add the nutmeg, sultanas, roasted nuts and poppy seeds and mix until smooth.

To bake in a breadmaker

Line the bread pan with baking parchment and spoon in the mixture. Set to bake only for 1 hour. Test the bread after about 45 minutes by pressing the top gently, if it springs back it is cooked. If not then it will need longer.

To bake by hand

Preheat the oven to 160°C (325°F), gas mark 3 and line a 1kg (2lb) loaf tin with baking parchment.

Pour the bread mixture into the prepared tin and bake in the preheated oven for 40–50 minutes until it is golden and firm on top when you press it gently in the middle.

Pressed focaccia

This bread knows how to survive life in the freezer – well, the refrigerator anyway. Perfect for a picnic served with a good selection of antipasti from your local deli.

INGREDIENTS

Homemade or leftover Focaccia (see recipe page 24), topped with rosemary sprigs and olives during baking

25ml (1fl oz) olive oil

6–8 roasted garlic cloves

200g (7oz) ricotta cheese

12 fresh basil leaves

100g (3½oz) roasted vegetables

2 handfuls baby spinach leaves

Salt and freshly ground black pepper

Here's how...

Cut the rosemary- and olive-topped focaccia in half lengthways and drizzle olive oil over one half of the bread. Squeeze the garlic cloves out of their skins and spread them over the same half.

Scatter the cheese, basil and vegetables evenly over the bread and top with the spinach leaves. Season with salt and pepper and top with the other half of the focaccia.

Wrap the loaf in cling film and place a large dinner plate on top with something heavy to press it down. Leave the focaccia overnight in the fridge to develop the flavours, then cut into slices to serve.

Chapter Five
Family

Toasted oven bottom muffins

Simple sourdough

Pizza

Pretzels for kids

Spring onion bagel

Irish soda farls

Hollowed-out ploughmans

Brioche filled with Nutella & roasted hazelnuts

Parmesan rolls

A family affair

Homemade bread is a kind of social glue. The family that makes bread together stays together? Something like that, I suppose.

I love spending time with my wife Emma, young daughter Poppy and her friends, tossing all sorts of ingredients into the breadmaker and throwing dough around the bread board. The look of wonderment on their faces as the finished bread comes out of the oven or breadmaker is a joy.

Make breadmaking fun and the kids get a lesson for life. The first thing I ever made at primary school was cheese on toasted bread. Later, when I was 14, I made my first-ever bread in my cooking class. I loved handling the flour, working the dough, it was so tactile and I could see it rising in the bowl. Afterwards, I threw the hot loaf in my rucksack and raced home shouting, 'Look what I've made?', and my mother found a squashed loaf nestling on a bed of crumbs!

We still laugh about my early breadmaking adventures to this day.

Toasted oven bottom muffins

A different take on traditional 'toast', this tasty Northern snack will brighten up a dull Sunday afternoon. They are very versatile and are equally suited to both sweet and savoury spreads and fillings.

INGREDIENTS

500g (1lb) strong white bread flour

1 tsp salt

1 tsp fast-action/easy-blend yeast

1 tsp granulated sugar

50ml (2fl oz) yogurt

250ml (8fl oz) milk

to serve

Fresh blueberries and lime zest, grated apple and cinnamon or cheese and roasted onions

Here's how... To make the dough in a breadmaker

Place all of the ingredients in the bread pan following the manufacturers' instructions regarding the order of liquid/dry ingredients and set your machine to the dough/pizza setting.

To make the dough by hand

Place the flour and salt in a mixing bowl and mix together the yeast, sugar, yogurt and milk in a measuring jug. Pour the liquid into the dry ingredients and using your hands, mix together until it forms a dough and comes away from the bowl – it should take about 3–4 minutes. Transfer the dough onto a lightly floured work surface and knead (see basic instructions on page 27) for about 5–10 minutes. Return the dough back to the bowl, cover with cling film and leave in a warm place for 30–40 minutes to double in size. Scoop the bread back out and give it a simple knead for 1 minute.

To finish

Turn out the dough onto a lightly floured work surface. Roll the dough out to about 2.5cm (1in) thick. Shape the muffins using a round cutter, re-rolling the excess dough to cut out the last few as needed. You should be able to make about 12 medium-sized muffins.

Preheat the oven to 180°C (350°F), gas mark 4.

Heat a dry frying pan and place the muffins into the pan 4–6 at a time depending on the size of your frying pan. Cook the muffins for about 3–4 minutes on each side until golden. Remove from the pan, place them onto a baking tray and bake in the preheated oven for a further 10 minutes.

Slice each muffin in half horizontally and top, spread or fill with your choice of ingredients.

Simple sourdough

Sourdough is the Holy Grail of breads – increasingly trendy to serve, but with a provenance stretching back in time. Crusty on the outside, chewy in the middle, I love it toasted and spread with a bitter orange marmalade.

INGREDIENTS

For the starter dough (see page 17)

1 tsp fast-action/easy-blend yeast

300g (10oz) strong white bread flour

2 tbsp balsamic vinegar

300ml (½ pint) water

1 tsp granulated sugar

For the bread

250g (8oz) sour starter dough

250g (8oz) strong white bread flour

1 tsp salt

1 tsp fast-action/easy-blend yeast

1 tsp granulated sugar

125ml (4fl oz) water

Here's how...

Mix the sour starter ingredients in a bowl, cover with a clean tea towel and secure with an elastic band. Leave for 12 hours to prove at room temperature. You will have enough starter dough for 2–3 loaves – you will only need one-third of it for this recipe. Keep the remainder in the refrigerator until needed, but every couple of days just add 1 tablespoon flour and 1 tablespoon water to keep it bubbling and alive.

To bake in a breadmaker

Place all of the ingredients in the bread pan following the manufacturers' instructions regarding the order of liquid/dry ingredients and set your machine to the French setting.

To bake by hand

Place the starter dough, flour and salt in a mixing bowl and mix together the yeast, sugar and water in a measuring jug. Pour the liquid into the dry ingredients and using your hands, mix together until it forms a dough and comes away from the bowl – it should take about 3–4 minutes. Transfer the dough onto a lightly floured work surface and knead (see basic instructions on page 27) for about 5–10 minutes. Return the dough back to the bowl, cover with cling film and leave in a warm place for 30–40 minutes to double in size. Scoop the bread back out and give it a simple knead for 1 minute.

Using your hands turn the dough under itself so you get a smooth top to the loaf. Place the dough into a 1kg (2lb) non-stick loaf tin or place it on a non-stick baking tray. Leave the bread to prove for another 20 minutes, until it doubles in size again. Meanwhile, preheat the oven to 200°C (400°F), gas mark 6.

Bake the loaf for 20–30 minutes until golden on top. To check if it is cooked, carefully slide the loaf out of the tin and tap the underneath. If it sounds hollow it is cooked, if not, return it to the oven for another 10 minutes.

Pizza

A classic Italian creation bursting with heady aromas and fresh Mediterranean flavours. Add your family's favourite toppings.

INGREDIENTS

For the sauce

10 ripe tomatoes

2 tsp salt

2 tsp granulated sugar

1 tbsp fresh chopped thyme

2 garlic cloves, crushed

1 tbsp olive oil

1 tbsp balsamic vinegar

For the dough

250g (8oz) strong white bread flour

250g (8oz) pasta flour

1 tsp salt

1 tsp fast-action/easy-blend yeast

1 tsp granulated sugar

300ml (½ pint) water

For the topping

2 mozzarella balls, sliced

10 fresh basil leaves, torn

Olives, Parma ham, roasted peppers, anchovies... whatever you fancy!

Here's how...

Preheat the oven to 160°C (325°F), gas mark 3. First, make the sauce. Halve the tomatoes, place them on a baking tray and sprinkle them with the salt, sugar, thyme and garlic. Drizzle with the oil and balsamic vinegar and place in the preheated oven for 30 minutes. Leave to cool for a further 30 minutes. Either blend the tomato mix until smooth in a food processor or press through a sieve. Set aside until needed.

To make the dough in a breadmaker

Place all of the dough ingredients in the bread pan following the manufacturers' instructions regarding the order of liquid/dry ingredients and set your machine to the dough/pizza setting.

To make the dough by hand

Place both of the flours and the salt in a mixing bowl and mix together the yeast, sugar and water in a measuring jug. Pour the liquid into the dry ingredients and using your hands, mix together until it forms a dough and comes away from the bowl – it should take about 3–4 minutes. Transfer the dough onto a lightly floured work surface and knead (see basic instructions on page 27) for about 5–10 minutes. Return the dough back to the bowl, cover with cling film and leave in a warm place for 30–40 minutes to double in size. Scoop the bread back out and give it a simple knead for 1 minute.

To finish

Preheat the oven to 200°C (400°F), gas mark 6 and also preheat 1–2 non-stick baking trays.

Turn the dough out onto a lightly floured work surface and divide it into six pieces. Roll each piece into circles about ½cm (¼in) thick and transfer them to the preheated baking tray(s). Spread a spoonful of the tomato sauce over the dough, top with the sliced mozzarella and torn basil leaves, and any other topping you have chosen. Bake in the oven for 12 minutes until golden brown.

Pretzels for kids

Too many bags of crisps is one of the dietary reasons our increasingly sedentary children are putting on weight. These pretzels are easy to make and keep well in an airtight container. You can also add different flavourings to this basic recipe, such as seeds, nuts or herbs as desired.

INGREDIENTS

500g (1lb) strong white bread flour

1 tsp salt

1 tsp fast-action/easy-blend yeast

1 tsp granulated sugar

275ml (9fl oz) water

1 egg, beaten (optional)

Here's how... To make the dough in a breadmaker

Place all of the ingredients, except the egg, in the bread pan following the manufacturers' instructions regarding the order of liquid/dry ingredients and set your machine to the dough/pizza setting.

To make the dough by hand

Place the flour and salt in a mixing bowl and mix together the yeast, sugar and water in a measuring jug. Pour the liquid into the dry ingredients and using your hands, mix together until it forms a dough and comes away from the bowl – it should take about 3–4 minutes. Transfer the dough onto a lightly floured work surface and knead (see basic instructions on page 27) for about 5–10 minutes. Return the dough back to the bowl, cover with cling film and leave in a warm place for 30–40 minutes to double in size. Scoop the bread back out and give it a simple knead for 1 minute.

To finish

Preheat the oven to 150°C (300°F), gas mark 2.

Turn the dough out onto a lightly floured work surface and cut the dough into 25g (1oz) balls (you should get about 30 in total). Roll the dough into long, thin strings and twist into pretzel shapes. Brush with the egg wash if using. Place the pretzels on a non-stick baking tray. Bake in the preheated oven for 35–40 minutes. Cool and store in an airtight container.

Spring onion bagel

Enjoy the ultimate comfort food with a nice mug of piping-hot tea or coffee. These oniony bagels are great cut in half, sprinkled with grated cheese and Worcestershire sauce and grilled until bubbling and golden.

INGREDIENTS

1 tbsp dried polenta

1 egg white, beaten

1 tbsp poppy seeds

For the dough

400g (13oz) strong white bread flour

1½ tsp salt

1½ tsp fast-action/easy-blend yeast

1 tbsp granulated sugar

225ml (7½fl oz) warm water

4 spring onions, chopped

Here's how... To make the dough in a breadmaker

Place all of the dough ingredients in the bread pan following the manufacturers' instructions regarding the order of liquid/dry ingredients and set your machine to the pizza/dough setting.

To make the dough by hand

Place the flour and salt in a mixing bowl and mix together the yeast, sugar, water and chopped spring onions in a measuring jug. Pour the liquid into the dry ingredients and using your hands, mix together until it forms a dough and comes away from the bowl – it should take about 3–4 minutes. Transfer the dough onto a lightly floured work surface and knead (see basic instructions on page 27) for about 5–10 minutes. Return the dough back to the bowl, cover with cling film and leave in a warm place for 30–40 minutes to double in size. Scoop the bread back out and give it a simple knead for 1 minute.

To finish

Turn the dough out onto a lightly floured work surface and allow to rest 20–30 minutes or until it has almost doubled in size. Meanwhile, preheat the oven to 190°C (375°F), gas mark 5 and grease a large baking tray.

Divide the dough into nine equal portions. Working quickly, shape each into a smooth ball. Punch a hole in the centre and pull gently to produce a 5cm (2in) hole. Place them on the prepared baking tray and sprinkle them with the polenta. Cover with oiled cling film and set aside for 10 minutes to rise (start timing after the first bagel is shaped).

Bring a large shallow pan of water to the boil, reduce to a simmer and place 3–4 bagels in at a time. Cook for 1 minute on each side then transfer them back to the greased baking tray.

Brush with the beaten egg white and sprinkle with poppy seeds. Bake in the preheated oven for 20–25 minutes until they are golden on top and sound hollow when tapped underneath.

Irish soda farls

Again, reflecting my ancestry, this is a quick breakfast dish which complements grilled pancetta, tomatoes and a poached free-range egg.

INGREDIENTS

450g (14oz) self-raising flour

1 tsp bicarbonate of soda

1 tsp salt

½ tsp ground white pepper

2 tbsp yogurt

50ml (2fl oz) vegetable oil

225ml (7½fl oz) milk

50g (2oz) ground semolina or polenta

Here's how...

Sieve the flour, bicarbonate of soda, salt and white pepper into a bowl. Make a well in the middle and pour in the yogurt, oil and milk. Stir the mixture together and add more milk, as required, to form a dough.

Divide the mixture into two equal parts. Dust your work surface with the semolina or polenta and roll each bit of dough out into flat 3–4cm (1½in) thick pancakes using the semolina or polenta to dust.

Preheat the oven to 180°C (350°F), gas mark 4 and place a dry frying pan over medium heat.

Cut the farls into quarters and cook for 3 minutes on each side until golden. Transfer them to a baking tray and bake them in the preheated oven for 15 minutes to finish cooking through.

Hollowed-out ploughmans

This is an eye-catching and eco-friendly way of serving this traditional dish, as you eat the container it comes in. Also makes for perfect picnic food.

INGREDIENTS

300g (10oz) granary flour

200g (7oz) plain wholemeal flour

1 tsp salt

1 tsp fast-action/easy-blend yeast

1 tsp granulated sugar

350ml (12fl oz) water

for the filling

A selection of different cheeses, meats, salad ingredients and pickles/relishes

Here's how... To make the dough in a breadmaker

Place all of the ingredients in the bread pan following the manufacturers' instructions regarding the order of liquid/dry ingredients and set your machine to the wholewheat dough setting.

To make the dough by hand

Place both the flours and salt in a mixing bowl and mix together the yeast, sugar and water in a measuring jug. Pour the liquid into the dry ingredients and using your hands, mix together until it forms a dough and comes away from the bowl – it should take about 3–4 minutes. Transfer the dough onto a lightly floured work surface and knead (see basic instructions on page 27) for about 5–10 minutes. Return the dough back to the bowl, cover with cling film and leave in a warm place for 30–40 minutes to double in size.

To finish

Turn the dough out onto a lightly floured work surface and knead the dough for several minutes. Shape into a round loaf, place onto a lined baking tray and leave to prove for 30 minutes. Meanwhile, preheat the oven to 200°C (400°F), gas mark 6.

Bake in the preheated oven for 30–40 minutes until it is golden and sounds hollow when tapped underneath. Leave to cool.

Cut the top off the loaf to make a lid and remove the soft crumb from the inside to create a container. Don't throw away the inside of your loaf – there are plenty of recipe ideas in the leftovers chapter (see pages 138–167).

Just before you are ready to go out fill the loaf with different cheeses, meats, salad ingredients and pickles or relishes. Replace the crust lid and wrap with a clean tea towel. Cut into slices to serve.

Brioche filled with Nutella & roasted hazelnuts

My take on pain au chocolat, this enriched, sweetened bread dough is delicious with a good-quality vanilla ice cream. Try to restrain yourself and don't eat the brioche straight from the oven as the chocolate will be molten hot.

INGREDIENTS

400g (13oz) strong white bread flour

½ tsp salt

125g (4oz) butter

1 tsp fast-action/easy-blend yeast

3 tbsp caster sugar

4 large eggs

25ml (2fl oz) milk

8 tbsp Nutella

50g (2oz) hazelnuts, roasted and chopped

Here's how... To make the dough in a breadmaker

Place all of the ingredients in the bread pan following the manufacturers' instructions regarding the order of liquid/dry ingredients and set your machine to the basic dough setting.

To make the dough by hand

Place the flour, salt and butter in a mixing bowl and mix together the yeast, sugar, eggs and milk in a measuring jug. Pour the liquid into the dry ingredients and using your hands, mix together until it forms a dough and comes away from the bowl – it should take about 3–4 minutes. Transfer the dough onto a lightly floured work surface and knead (see basic instructions on page 27) for about 5–10 minutes. Return the dough back to the bowl, cover with cling film and leave in a warm place for 30–40 minutes to double in size.

To finish

Turn the dough out onto a lightly floured work surface and knead the dough for 1 minute. Divide the dough into 10 equal portions. Roll out each piece into a circle about 10–15cm (4–6in)and place a spoonful of Nutella into the centre along with a sprinkling of roasted hazelnuts. Bring all the sides of the dough together in the centre and press them to create a seal.

Place the rolls sealed-side down on a lined baking tray and leave to prove for 30 minutes. Meanwhile, preheat the oven to 190°C (375°F), gas mark 5.

Bake the brioche in the preheated oven for 20–30 minutes or until golden brown on top.

Parmesan rolls

I like to serve these breads filled with a local dry-cured ham and some dressed rocket leaves. Simple, unpretentious food.

INGREDIENTS

500g (1lb) strong white bread flour

1¼ tsp salt

1 tsp fast-action/easy-blend yeast

1½ tsp granulated sugar

300ml (½ pint) water

25g (1oz) butter or 25ml (1fl oz) oil

100g (3½oz) Parmesan cheese, plus extra for sprinkling

2 egg yolks, beaten

Here's how... To make the dough in a breadmaker

Place all of the ingredients, except the Parmesan and egg yolks, in the bread pan following the manufacturers' instructions regarding the order of liquid/dry ingredients and set your machine to the dough/pizza setting.

To make the dough by hand

Place the flour and salt in a mixing bowl and mix together the yeast, sugar, and water in a measuring jug. Pour the liquid into the dry ingredients and using your hands, mix together until it forms a dough and comes away from the bowl – it should take about 3–4 minutes. Transfer the dough onto a lightly floured work surface and knead (see basic instructions on page 27) for about 5–10 minutes. Return the dough back to the bowl, cover with cling film and leave in a warm place for 30–40 minutes to double in size. Scoop the bread back out and give it a simple knead for 1 minute.

To finish

Turn the dough out onto a lightly floured work surface and roll it into a rectangle about 1cm (½in) thick. Grate the Parmesan evenly over the dough.

Brush the long side nearest you with some beaten egg yolk and roll the dough from the back towards you to make a Swiss roll. Cut the dough into 4cm (1½in) slices and place them cut-side down on a lined baking tray.

Brush with some more beaten egg yolk and leave to prove for 20 minutes or until they have doubled in size. Meanwhile, preheat the oven to 200°C (400°F), gas mark 6.

When the rolls have doubled in size, sprinkle over some extra Parmesan before transferring them to the preheated oven for 20 minutes until they are golden on top and sound hollow when tapped underneath.

Chapter Six
Leftovers

Waste not, want not

At last our throw-away society is in retreat. More and more of us are throwing less and less away. Never discard two-day-old bread that has gone slightly hard. Toast it for crostinis, make croutons for soup or salads or dip slices into beaten egg and fry. Also, a classic bread and butter pudding takes no time at all.

Still got some hard crusts left over? Take the kids to the local park and help them feed the ducks. An old loaf packed with seeds will even be good for the birds.

I love collecting cooking and baking tips. I never usually write them down but prefer to simply remember them in my head. This final section breaks the habit of a lifetime! It is full of handy hints and advice on how to get terrific results. Through trial and error and listening to other bakers I have discovered how to get the best out of bread. I am delighted to pass them on.

Moroccan roast chicken

This is a simple fresh take on the traditional roast chicken dinner, but I have introduced the amazing combination of flavours from Morocco. This dish would be great served up with some saffron potatoes and green beans cooked in tomatoes.

SERVES 4

INGREDIENTS

1 tsp cumin seeds

1 tsp coriander seeds

50g (2oz) pistachios

1 large white onion, finely chopped

100g (3½oz) breadcrumbs

1 handful fresh coriander leaves, chopped

1 handful fresh mint leaves, chopped

1 lemon (preserved in salt if you can get it), finely chopped

1 large egg, beaten

1 large free-range chicken, weighing about 1kg (2lb)

Olive oil, for drizzling

Salt and freshly ground black pepper

Here's how...

Preheat the oven to 180°C (350°F), gas mark 4.

Put the cumin and coriander seeds into a non-stick frying pan and toast the seeds over a medium heat until they start to crackle. Remove the seeds and place them in a mortar. Put the pan back on the heat and add the pistachios. Continue to toast until they take on a nutty golden colour. Remove from the heat and place into a bowl.

Add the onion, breadcrumbs and chopped herbs to the bowl with the pistachios. Crush the toasted spices in the mortar with the pestle – I like to leave them a little coarse so there is some texture – and add them to the bowl (reserving a little) along with the preserved lemon. Season with salt and pepper.

Add in the beaten egg and get your hands in to mix the stuffing until it starts to come together. Spoon the stuffing into the chicken until it is about half full.

Place the chicken on a roasting tray and drizzle a little olive oil over the top. Season with salt, pepper and the reserved coriander and cumin seeds. Pour 600ml (1 pint) of water into the bottom of the roasting dish. Cook the chicken for 1½ hours until completely cooked through.

Crumbs! Follow these simple tips for perfect breadcrumbs:

Homemade breadcrumbs are easy to make, improve the taste of many dishes and are much cheaper than shop-bought. Store in a resealable plastic bag in the freezer and use as required.

- Use any type of bread and even combine different types for some wonderful taste experiences.
- Use dry bread for perfect results. If your bread is too fresh and moist, bake fresh bread slices in a slow oven for a few minutes. Never use stale bread or you will get horrible stale-tasting breadcrumbs.
- Save spare bread slices and ends of bread in a large resealable plastic bag in the freezer until you have enough to make your breadcrumbs.
- To make breadcrumbs, place pieces of bread in a food processor and whizz until you reach a coarse mix.

Poor man's Parmesan

When you fancy a tasty quick pasta dish and there's no Parmesan or ingredients for sauce, don't despair. This rescue recipe will change the way you eat pasta – guaranteed.

SERVES 2

INGREDIENTS

150g (5oz) good-quality dried pasta

4 tbsp fine breadcrumbs (see page 142)

1 small red chilli, deseeded and finely chopped

2 anchovies in oil, chopped

2 garlic cloves, finely chopped

2 tbsp extra virgin olive oil, plus a little extra for mixing

Freshly ground black pepper

Here's how...

Put a large pan of salted water on to boil. Add the pasta and cook for about 9–12 minutes or until al dente.

Place the breadcrumbs, chilli, anchovies and garlic into a food processor and blend to a fine crumb.

Pour the olive oil into a frying pan and cook the breadcrumb mixture over a gentle heat until golden and crispy.

When the pasta is cooked to taste, drain but retain some of the cooking water as the starch helps the consistency of the finished sauce.

Put the drained pasta back into the cooking pan with a little of the retained cooking water. Add a generous splash of extra virgin olive oil, mix in the crispy breadcrumbs and serve with a good twist of black pepper.

Herb-crusted salmon

Breadcrumbs, herbs, salmon – herb-crusted salmon it is! An rich and tasty fish, this recipe is a perennial favourite in my household.

SERVES 2

INGREDIENTS

25g (1oz) mixed fresh herbs (rosemary, chervil, basil), chopped

Freshly grated zest of 1 lemon

100g (3½oz) breadcrumbs (see page 142)

75g (3oz) butter

2 x 225g (7½oz) fresh salmon fillets

Salt and freshly ground black pepper

Here's how...

Preheat the oven to 180°C (350°F), gas mark 4.

Place the chopped fresh herbs, lemon zest, breadcrumbs, butter and some salt and pepper into a food processor and pulse to mix.

Scoop the mixture out onto a piece of baking parchment or cling film and press the mixture down. Place another piece of parchment over the top and roll out the mixture to about ½cm (¼in) thick. Peel off the top layer of parchment revealing an even crust.

Place the salmon fillets skin-side up onto the crust. Cut around the fish, lift them off the parchment (salmon and crust) and transfer them to a baking tray placing the fillets skin-side down.

Bake the salmon in the preheated oven for about 12 minutes until the crust is golden.

Chorizo salad

This salad doesn't last long at the table in my house. Meaty and satisfying, it's equally at home in hot weather and cold, and will bring a bit of Mediterranean flavour to your home.

SERVES 4

INGREDIENTS

300g (10oz) chorizo

½ ciabatta (see page 80)

1 handful of fresh coriander

3 baby Gem lettuce

25ml (1fl oz) sherry vinegar

100ml (3½fl oz) extra virgin olive oil, plus extra for drizzling

Here's how...

Preheat the oven to 150°C (300°F), gas mark 2.

Chop the chorizo and the ciabatta into chunks, transfer to a roasting tray and drizzle with a little olive oil. Bake in the preheated oven for 40 minutes until the croutons are crisp. Remove from the oven and leave to cool to room temperature.

Roughly chop the coriander, core the lettuce, cut into quarters and add to the croutons, mixing well. Transfer into a large salad bowl.

In a measuring jug whisk together the vinegar and olive oil to taste, pour over the salad and serve.

The ultimate toastie

Just like skiing is the ultimate sporting high for me, this take on a sandwich is the ultimate toastie. I always make it on my annual ski trip to France.

SERVES 1

INGREDIENTS

2 slices of leftover white bread

25g (1oz) butter

2 slices dry-cured ham

1 tsp Dijon mustard

1 tbsp mascarpone

2 sprigs thyme

Freshly ground black pepper

Here's how...

Butter the bread and turn it over, butter-side down. Lay a slice of dry-cured ham on each slice of bread.

Spread the mustard on one slice and mascarpone on the other. Season to taste with black pepper and a few sprigs of thyme.

Sandwich the bread butter-side out and place into a dry frying pan over a low heat. Cook on each side for about 5 minutes or until the toastie is golden on both sides.

Cinnamon toast

This sweet toast is perfect served with barbecued plums or a good plum compote. Top with a dollop of crème fraîche and a dusting of icing sugar to round it off.

SERVES 1

INGREDIENTS

2 large free-range eggs

1 tbsp icing sugar

1 tsp of ground cinnamon

½ vanilla pod

50g (2oz) butter

2 slices leftover white bread

Here's how...

Break the eggs into a bowl, add the icing sugar and cinnamon and whisk together.

Cut the vanilla pod lengthways and using a knife scrape the inside of the pod to release the vanilla seeds and add them to the bowl, mixing well.

Heat a dry frying pan and add the butter.

Dip the bread into the sweetened egg mixture, ensuring that the slices are well coated.

Place the bread into the frying pan and cook on each side for 3–4 minutes or until golden.

Parmesan-crusted chicken

Served with slow-roasted vine tomatoes, the contrasting flavours and texture are simply superb and really complete the meal.

SERVES 4

INGREDIENTS

4 chicken breasts, skinned and pounded until 1cm (½in) thick

2 eggs, beaten

1 tablespoon milk

200g (7oz) breadcrumbs (see page 142)

50g (2oz) grated Parmesan

50g (2oz) plain flour

Olive oil

Sea salt and freshly ground black pepper

Here's how...

Preheat the oven to 180°C (350°F), gas mark 4.

Season the chicken fillets on both sides with a little salt and pepper.

Lightly beat the eggs together with the milk in a shallow bowl. Mix the breadcrumbs with the Parmesan in a separate bowl.

Dust each chicken breast escalope in flour, dip into the beaten eggs and finally coat with the Parmesan breadcrumbs.

Heat some olive oil in a frying pan over a medium heat and fry the escalopes for about 2 minutes on each side or until browned.

Drain the cooked chicken on kitchen paper, then transfer to a baking tray and cook in the preheated oven for a further 12 minutes.

Egg bango

This recipe was inspired by a friend of mine who I first saw making it with one arm in a sling after breaking his collarbone on a ski trip. I used both my hands to make this but imagine how hard it would be to make this with just one functioning arm.

SERVES 1

INGREDIENTS

2 slices of leftover white bread

25g (1oz) butter

2 tbsp oil

1 free-range egg

Freshly ground black pepper

Here's how...

Butter the bread on both sides and place under a preheated grill, toasting on both sides.

Heat the oil in a frying pan and cook the egg gently, to taste. Place the egg between the toasted slices and season with black pepper.

Apple strudel toastie

I always ensure that I have some leftover brioche to make this fantastic, simple toastie. Not as Austrian as the Habsburgs but delicious nonetheless.

SERVES 1

INGREDIENTS

2 tbsp apple sauce

1 tbsp sultanas

½ tsp mixed spice

½ tsp brown sugar

A few shavings of lemon zest

2 slices of leftover brioche

25g (1oz) butter

Good-quality ice cream or single cream, to serve

Here's how...

In a bowl mix together the apple sauce, sultanas, mixed spice, sugar and lemon zest.

Spread one side of each slice of brioche with butter and turn them over, butter-side down.

Spoon the spiced mixture onto one slice of the bread and place the other slice on top butter-side up.

Preheat the grill or a toasted sandwich maker and when it reaches the right temperature place the sandwich in to toast. Serve with some good ice cream or single cream.

Honey & lavender tart

A great use of lavender that works particularly well with sweet honey. My wife Emma always dries a few bags of lavender to use in the kitchen.

SERVES 8

INGREDIENTS

For the pastry

250g (8oz) plain flour, plus extra for dusting

50g (2oz) icing sugar

125g (4oz) chilled butter, cut into cubes

1 free-range egg, lightly beaten

For the filling

100g (3½oz) leftover bread

1 tsp dried lavender

50g (2oz) butter

250g (8oz) golden syrup

100g (3½oz) local runny honey

1 lemon, zest and juice

1 large free-range egg

50ml (2fl oz) double cream

Here's how...

Prepare the pastry by sifting the flour and icing sugar into a bowl. Use your fingertips to rub in the butter until the mixture resembles fine breadcrumbs. Add the egg and mix well to form a dough and chill in the refrigerator for 30 minutes.

Preheat the oven to 180°C (350°F), gas mark 4.

Roll the pastry dough out to 2mm (⅛in) thick and use to line a 20cm (8in) round tart tin. Fill with baking beans and blind bake in the preheated oven for 15 minutes, or until the pastry is golden brown, removing the beans during the last 5 minutes of baking. Allow to cool. Reduce the oven temperature to 160°C (325°F), gas mark 3.

Meanwhile, make the filling. Place the bread and the lavender into a food processor and pulse to fine breadcrumbs.

Heat the butter in a pan until browned. Gently warm the golden syrup, honey, lemon juice and zest in a separate pan and stir in the browned butter.

Mix the egg and cream until well combined. Pour the golden syrup mixture into the combined eggs and cream and stir in the prepared breadcrumbs.

Pour the mixture into the cooked tart case and bake in the oven for 25 minutes. Turn the oven temperature down to 140°C (275°F), gas mark 1 and bake for a further 20 minutes, or until the tart is golden brown and bubbling. Remove from the oven and leave to cool before turning out.

Salsa verde

This is a superior alternative to traditional mint sauce. I think it works better as it cuts through the richness of the lamb. This recipe will make 1 x 250ml (8fl oz) jar.

INGREDIENTS

½ **red onion**

¼ **garlic clove**

1 tsp **Dijon mustard**

4 tbsp **red wine vinegar**

8 tbsp **olive oil**

2 **large handfuls of fresh mint, chopped**

1 **handful of fresh parsley, chopped**

1 **slice of leftover white bread, cubed**

1 tsp **granulated sugar (optional)**

Salt and freshly ground black pepper, to taste

Here's how...

Finely chop the red onion and garlic and place in a bowl with the mustard, vinegar and olive oil. Add the chopped herbs and season to taste with salt and pepper.

Add the bread cubes and leave to stand for 20 minutes, allowing the bread to soak up all the flavours. Taste, adding the sugar and adjusting the seasoning if desired.

Serve with roast lamb. Use any leftovers to add a zing to tomato salads or sandwiches. Store in a sterilised jar in the fridge for 1–2 weeks.

Panzanella salad

Lots of my favourite Mediterranean ingredients combine to produce a heavenly salad that everyone loves.

SERVES 4

INGREDIENTS

300g (10oz) leftover bread, torn into bite-sized pieces

125ml (4fl oz) olive oil, plus extra for drizzling

3 garlic cloves, finely chopped

1 red pepper

1 yellow pepper

25ml (1fl oz) balsamic vinegar

500g (1lb) ripe cherry tomatoes, cut into quarters

125g (4oz) sliced red onion

10 fresh basil leaves, shredded

75g (3oz) green olives, pitted and halved

25g (1oz) pine nuts, toasted (optional)

Salt and freshly ground black pepper

Here's how...

Preheat the oven to 200°C (400°F), gas mark 6.

In a large bowl, toss the bread with 75ml (3½fl oz) olive oil, garlic and some salt and pepper. Transfer the seasoned bread to a baking sheet, and toast in the preheated oven until golden, about 5-10 minutes; remove from the oven and leave to cool slightly.

Chop the peppers into chunks, drizzle with a little olive oil, add salt and pepper and place on a preheated grill pan for 5 minutes until you get some really nice grill marks.

Whisk together the remaining olive oil and balsamic vinegar. Gently toss together the crispy bread, tomatoes, onion, basil, olives and peppers. Toss with the vinaigrette and allow to stand for 20 minutes before serving. You might like to add a handful of toasted pine nuts before taking to the table, too.

Duck bread

Sometimes there is nothing else for it. Grab a little quality time with your loved ones and go and feed the ducks. It does not matter how many times I take my daughter to the edge of Derwent Water lake to feed the ducks, she just loves it. I guess it's the simple things in life that can sometimes be the most pleasurable. So, next time you get to the bottom of the bread bin and there's only the crusts left, think of the ducks and take a little time out so they can benefit from your baking, too.

INGREDIENTS

Any unwanted bread, but loaves containing seeds are particularly good

Here's how...

Remove stale, unwanted bread from the bread bin. Place into a reusable carrier bag.

Walk to the local park, children in tow. Break the bread into small pieces and toss to the ducks.

Smile and think how good life is...

Index

Index

Acknowledgements

I would like to thank my fantastic wife Emma and beautiful daughter Poppy for their love and support. Without them I would not be able to achieve half of what I set out to do.

Thanks also to all my parents and in-laws for all their ongoing help and encouragement.

A special thank you goes to my fantastic team at Good Taste – Kylie Overton, Dan Grimshaw, Becca Newton, Ali Burlington and Edoardo Gren – who have all helped in their own special ways to make sure I was able to commit the time and energy to this book. Thanks also to my friends James, Fiona and Jack Breedon for the loan of their kitchen.

Finally, I am grateful to Panasonic for their guidance in helping me to get the best out of automatic breadmakers, and also to Carr's Flour for their generous donations of excellent flour!

Peter Sidwell

Conversion tables

Approximate European/American conversion

	Metric	Imperial	USA
Breadcrumbs	50g	2oz	1 cup
Brown sugar	170g	6oz	1 cup
Butter	115g	4oz	1 cup
Butter/margarine/lard	225g	8oz	1 cup
Castor and granulated sugar	225g	8oz	1 cup
Currants	140g	5oz	1 cup
Flour	140g	5ox	1 cup
Golden Syrup	350g	12oz	1 cup
Ground almonds	115g	4oz	1 cup
Hazelnuts, whole	150g	5oz	1 cup
Herbs, chopped	25g	1oz	1 cup
Oats	25g	1oz	1 cup
Sultanas/raisins	200g	7oz	1 cup

Liquid Measurements

5ml	1 tsp
15ml	1 tbsp or ½ fl oz
25ml	1fl oz
50ml	2fl oz or ¼ cup
75ml	3fl oz
100ml	3½fl oz
125ml	4fl oz or ½ cup
150ml	5fl oz (¼ pint)
175ml	6fl oz
200ml	7fl oz
225ml	7½fl oz
250ml	8fl oz or 1 cup
275ml	9fl oz
300ml	½ pint or 1¼ cups
450ml	¾ pint
600ml	1 pt (20 fl oz)
1 litre	1¾ pints

Weights

15g	½oz	400g	13oz
25g	1oz	450g	14oz
50g	2oz	475g	15oz
75g	3oz	500g	1lb
100g	3½oz	675g	1¼lb
125g	4oz	750g	1½lb
150g	5oz	1kg	2lb
175g	6oz	1.25kg	2½lb
200g	7oz	1.5kg	3lb
225g	7½oz	1.75kg	3½lb
250g	8oz	2kg	4lb
275g	9oz		
300g	10oz		
375g	11oz		

Oven temperatures

°C	°F	Gas Mark	Oven
110	225	¼	
120	250	½	
140	275	1	Cool
150	300	2	
160	325	3	Moderate
180	350	4	
190	375	5	Moderately Hot
200	400	6	
220	425	7	Hot
230	450	8	
240	475	9	Very Hot

NB Cooking times for fan assisted ovens may be shorter. Please refer to manufacturers guidelines. All conversions are approximate.